The Family-Friendly KETO Instant Pot® Cookbook

DELICIOUS, LOW-CARB MEALS YOU CAN HAVE ON THE TABLE QUICKLY & EASILY

ANNA HUNLEY

Creator of Keto in Pearls

FAIR WINDS

Inspiring | Educating | Creating | Entertaining

Brimming with creative inspiration, how-to projects, and useful information to enrich your everyday life, Quarto Knows is a favorite destination for those pursuing their interests and passions. Visit our site and dig deeper with our books into your area of interest: Quarto Creates, Quarto Cooks, Quarto Homes, Quarto Lives, Quarto Drives, Quarto Explores, Quarto Gifts, or Quarto Kids.

First Published in 2019 by Fair Winds Press, an imprint of The Quarto Group, 100 Cummings Center, Suite 265-D, Beverly, MA 01915, USA.
T (978) 282-9590 F (978) 283-2742 QuartoKnows.com

Fair Winds Press titles are also available at discount for retail, wholesale, promotional, and bulk purchase. For details, contact the Special Sales Manager by email at specialsales@quarto.com or by mail at The Quarto Group, Attn: Special Sales Manager, 100 Cummings Center, Suite 265-D, Beverly, MA 01915, USA.

23 22 21 20 19   1 2 3 4 5

ISBN: 978-1-59233-889-4

Digital edition published in 2019
eISBN: 978-1-63159-753-4

Library of Congress Cataloging-in-Publication Data

Hunley, Anna, author.
The family-friendly keto Instant Pot cookbook : delicious, low-carb
  meals you can have on the table quickly & easily / Anna Hunley.
ISBN 9781631597534 (ebook) | ISBN 9781592338894 (pbk.)
1. Reducing diets--Recipes. 2. Low-carbohydrate diet--Recipes.
  3. Ketogenic diet--Recipes. 4. Quick and easy cooking. 5. Smart cookers.
LCC RM222.2 (ebook) | LCC RM222.2 .H8565 2019 (print)
DDC 641.5/6383--dc23

LCCN 2019006759 (print) | LCCN 2019007891 (ebook)

Design: Laura Klynstra
Photography: Art Noodles Studio LLC, except those by Natalie Morgan (page 195) and Shutterstock (pages 4, 6, 10, 26, 32, 44, 58, 76, 90, 112, 152, 174)

Printed in China

The information in this book is for educational purposes only. It is not intended to replace the advice of a physician or medical practitioner. Please see your health-care provider before beginning any new health program.

For

Harper Grace, Cooper, and Norah

There are not enough waves in the ocean

to express my love for you.

Contents

Introduction 7

Chapter 1:
Keto Crash Course 10

   The Basics 12

   How It Works 12

   What Exactly Can You Eat? 13

      Fat: The Lever 13

      Protein: The Goal 14

      Carbohydrates: The Limit 14

   Bonus Recipes 16

   Keto Sweeteners 21

   Keto + Kids 21

   Let's Go Shopping 22

   Keto on a Budget 23

   What a Full Day of
   Eating Keto Looks Like 24

Chapter 2:
Get to Know Your Instant Pot 26

   Functionality 28

   Accessories for Your Instant Pot 30

   Caring for Your Instant Pot 31

Chapter 3:
Breaking Your Fast 32

Chapter 4:
Appetizers and Party Snacks 44

Chapter 5:
Soups, Stews, and Chilis 58

Chapter 6:
Covered Dishes 76

Chapter 7:
Beef 90

Chapter 8:
Poultry, Pork, and Seafood 112

Chapter 9:
Side Dishes 152

Chapter 10:
Desserts 174

Resources 192
Acknowledgments 193
About the Author 195
Index 196

Introduction

For as long as I can remember, my life has revolved around food. We celebrated birthdays at nice restaurants, rewarded achievements with trips to the local ice cream shop, and forgot bad days over giant bowls of pasta. Growing up in the Deep South, nearly everything was deep-fried, extra sweet, and extra large. It's just the Southern way of life.

My mother is a fabulous cook. There weren't many evenings that passed without all four of us gathered around the dinner table at 6 p.m. enjoying a home-cooked meal. Still, processed food was abundant. Bless their hearts, our parents just didn't know any better at the time. Processed foods and hormone-laced meats didn't carry the stigma that they do today. Low-fat diets and meal-replacement shakes were all the rage in the '90s. It wasn't until the early to mid-2000s that people started waking up to the danger that is processed food!

Unknowingly, that processed food began taking its toll on me. My issues with food and body image emerged during my adolescence. My recollection of first feeling ashamed of my body occurred when I was around ten years old. I remember a trip to the mall with my mom in search of a new pair of jeans. Nothing in the girl's department fit me properly, so we bought a pair of boy's husky-size jeans.

I hated those jeans. It was the first time in my life I ever felt embarrassed about the way I looked. Although I was only in elementary school at the time, that pair of jeans made a profound impact on my future.

As I matured, I found pleasure and enjoyment in food—and also the restaurants, the experiences, and the company. As with many young people (and old alike), I began this habit of catering to my every whim. Indulgence became my middle name. I ate what I wanted, when I wanted, and however much I wanted. It didn't bother me if I felt ill after eating too much as long as the food satisfied me emotionally. When I went off to college, I gained more than just the "freshman 15," and by the time I was twenty-two, I was pushing 200 pounds (91 kg) on a 5'3" (160 cm) frame. I am still an indulgent person, and this habit of self-gratification is something I will probably have to be cognizant of for the rest of my life.

My eating habits led me down a rabbit hole of uncontrolled weight gain. After marriage and two children, I reached my heaviest weight of 250 pounds (113 kg), and I wasn't even thirty years old. If I'm being perfectly honest, that number might actually have been higher, but at the time I didn't dare step on a scale to face reality. To say I was constantly tired, irritable, unhappy, and ashamed is an understatement.

A TURNING POINT

When I saw our Christmas photos in 2016, I knew that 2017 would be the year to make lasting changes. I was sick and tired of being sick and tired. I wanted to teach my children how to have a healthy relationship with food, and that meant leading by example.

Oddly enough, I first learned about the ketogenic diet on Instagram. The weight loss I observed in people following a ketogenic lifestyle blew me away. I was ready to sign up as soon as I realized bacon and cheese were acceptable food choices! (I'm kidding. Kind of.)

I spent about a month researching the lifestyle prior to adopting it as my own. Understanding *why* the body favors a ketogenic diet over other ways of eating was really important to me. In early 2017, I threw out everything in our refrigerator and pantry and never looked back. I was all in!

Keto came with its own set of challenges, though. Adopting a mostly grain-free, gluten-free, and zero-sugar diet meant I had some *unlearning* to do. Nearly everything I knew about cooking and baking no longer

worked. (Who knew that taking gluten out of a cake was a big deal?) As I navigated my way through a kitchen devoid of flour and sugar, I started blogging about my culinary creations and experiences—while involving my family in the ketogenic lifestyle.

Did you know that pearls start to form from one single grain of sand? I called my blog Keto in Pearls because I felt like my life was the soon-to-be pearl, and keto was my grain of sand. I was creating something beautiful and strong from the smallest of changes. Let's be honest, everything looks good with pearls. #CanIgetanamen? It didn't take me long to realize there were other ladies all over the world who needed help in their own kitchens. My blog was for moms, and dads, who felt like serving low-carb and sugar-free food to their families was a never-ending battle. I felt a calling to encourage other mommas (and daddies!) and wives as they navigated this new way of eating in their homes. After all, it takes a village.

KETO IS FUSS FREE AND FAMILY FRIENDLY!

As I mentioned, my children's future played a vital role in my decision to adopt a keto diet. For this way of eating to be sustainable, though, I needed to get the entire family on board. Short-order cook isn't in my job description. When I develop recipes, I write for parents like me, the ones who struggle to get their kids to eat what they put on the table. (One hour of supper has the ability to really challenge my salvation!) All the recipes in this book, and on my blog, are family friendly. Each recipe has been tested and approved by my picky husband and overtly honest children. If they don't give a recipe the thumbs up, I don't publish it.

If your family is anything like mine, your calendar is busting at the seams. Just the idea of cooking a full meal on an already jam-packed day seems daunting and dreadful. Thankfully, eating a ketogenic diet doesn't mean you need to slave away over the stove for two hours only to eat for ten minutes and spend the next forty doing dishes. Phew, I'm tired after just writing that! My goal with this cookbook is to show you how to make delicious, keto-friendly meals more efficiently with only one pot to clean up!

If you're feeling overwhelmed, don't. Along with 100 down-home recipes, in this book I give you:

- A brief overview of the ketogenic diet and its health benefits, along with keto buzzwords
- Ways to replace non-keto-friendly foods with keto-friendly ones
- Ideas to help your children eat cleaner, low-carb snacks
- Ways to save money and stay within a budget at the grocery store
- Step-by-step instructions for using your Instant Pot

All my recipes are sugar free, low carb, and predominantly gluten free. (If a recipe does contain an ingredient that isn't gluten free, I offer substitutions.) Most recipes also include the breakdown of macronutrients, meal pairing suggestions, and helpful tips for guaranteed cooking success. I have faith that you are equipped with everything you need to have a fruitful ketogenic lifestyle!

If you're brand spankin' new to keto, you might be wondering what a typical day of eating keto looks like. Or perhaps you're not new to eating keto but wonder whether it's possible to use only the recipes in this book to plan your meals. Because I want so badly for you to succeed, I've put together a few menus in chapter 1 for you to see that not only is a full day of keto easy and delicious, but you can also do it using only the recipes in this book!

I've always believed that life happens over food. When we sit around a table with the ones we love, conversation flows and relationships deepen. This is why I wanted to write this cookbook. Spend the time you save in the kitchen by playing a game with your family, going for a walk, or enjoying a new activity together! These recipes are my gift to you. I aim to serve my fellow keto families by making your ketogenic lifestyle sustainable. I pray that this cookbook allows your family to spend time around the table, enjoying a no-fuss, home-cooked meal and making memories together because at the end of the day, all that really matters is our family and our health.

In Love and Grace,

Anna

Keto Crash Course

L et's talk about one of my favorite topics in the whole world: keto! The ketogenic lifestyle, or keto (pronounced key-toe) diet, as it is commonly called, continues to grow in popularity across the United States and globally. Developed in the 1940s as a remedy for epileptic patients, the ketogenic diet became mainstream at the turn of the twenty-first century. In 2018, the attention centered on keto outshined any other popular diet/lifestyle, including the Paleo, Whole30, and Atkins diets. When compared to its rivals, a ketogenic diet is the optimal choice because it focuses on fueling the body with fat instead of glucose.

THE BASICS

In a nutshell, the term *ketogenic* means keeping your body in a state of nutritional ketosis, making it rely on fat instead of glucose (sugar) for energy. To do this, you must restrict your carbohydrate and glucose intake.

When you restrict your carbohydrates to a very low amount, typically fewer than 50 grams of carbs per day (though most people limit it to fewer than 20 grams), your liver starts producing magical gems called ketones. These ketones are your fuel source when you are in nutritional ketosis, or are "fat adapted." This means that your body is efficiently burning fat (ketones) instead of glucose for energy.

So why would you want to stay in nutritional ketosis? There are several reasons, but here are the top three:

1. **The brain works most efficiently when you consume fat instead of glucose for energy.** You will feel more alert and experience less brain fog throughout the day. No more 2 p.m. sugar crash!

2. **You will experience a naturally suppressed appetite.** When you eat a low-carb, high-fat diet and your body is burning ketones, you will find that you do not need as much to eat in a day as you did when you were a glucose burner. No more cravings or ravenous feelings!

3. **You'll probably lose weight.** When your body is burning fat (ketones) for energy, it first uses the fat that has been consumed through food. When it uses up all that fat, it then burns the fat stores within the body (that is, "extra" fat), resulting in weight loss for you!

There are other health reasons people might start following a ketogenic diet. People with type II diabetes, polycystic ovary syndrome, migraines, anxiety, and high blood pressure have been able to successfully manage their conditions by making a few simple adjustments to adopt a keto diet.

HOW IT WORKS

The three main components of a ketogenic diet are **fats**, **proteins**, and **carbohydrates**. Together, these make up your macronutrients, or "macros" for short. A ketogenic diet is a high-fat, moderate-protein, low-carbohydrate diet. Most people tend to follow a 75-20-5 ratio,

HOW I CALCULATED MACROS FOR THIS BOOK

Macros were calculated using a fitness app and the U.S. Department of Agriculture (USDA) Food Composition Database. Vegetables were weighed after paring (i.e., trimming and dicing). The figures provided for bone-in proteins, such as the Garlic-Parmesan Chicken Wings on page 51, are averages based on data from the USDA. All the nutritional information is intended as a guide, and you should calculate your own macros using a fitness app to ensure the most accurate information based on the weights and brands you consume.

meaning that 75 percent of their macros comes from fat, 20 percent comes from protein, and 5 percent comes from carbohydrates. Of course, these numbers can fluctuate depending on your body type, activity level, age, gender, and so on, but thankfully, calculating your macro needs isn't as tricky as it sounds. There are several free resources on the Internet to help you get started. Search "keto macro calculator" to calculate your specific macro requirements.

It's important to note that calories are not the be-all and end-all on keto. While the most important factor is your carbohydrate consumption, that's not to say that calories *don't* matter. On the contrary, the fact remains that you *must* be in a calorie deficit to lose weight. Though it's important to stay within a range for your body type, consuming slightly more calories occassionally will not derail your state of ketosis.

WHAT EXACTLY CAN YOU EAT?

This is naturally the first question people ask. If you were to ask a non-keto person what they thought someone following a ketogenic diet eats, their response would probably include bacon, butter, and avocados. This assumption leads people to believe that a ketogenic diet avoids all nutrient-rich foods.

In reality, a keto diet is centered around macronutrients. The goal with keto is to eat whole and clean foods that meet the only requirement of being low carb. Unlike in other diets, a list of "keto-approved foods" is nonexistent. That said, my motto is that if you

HOW TO AVOID THE KETO FLU

When you're first entering ketosis and withdrawing from sugar, your body reacts much in the same way as it would if you were detoxing from drugs. Your body releases more water than it stores because the pancreas is creating less insulin. (This is a good thing!) You might develop migraines, sweats, chills, fatigue, stomach pain, digestive problems, and mood swings. Thankfully, you can avoid these symptoms by consuming enough electrolytes. You can increase your electrolytes by consuming more sodium (salt), potassium (found in avocado, salmon, and other foods), sugar-free sports drinks, and sole water, or by supplementation. Last but not least, drink lots of water! If your urine is pale in color or clear, you are hydrated.

make the best choices 90 percent of the time, then the other 10 percent can be your buffer. This means you're not forbidden from eating a hot dog ever again!

Fat: The Lever

Contrary to popular belief, healthy fats such as those found in avocados, nuts, and eggs generally improve cholesterol levels and lower the risk of heart disease. You may experience sticker shock the first time you calculate your macros and see that you need to consume more than 100 grams of fat per day, but don't fret!

Think of your fat macros as a lever. You can pull that lever all the way down on days when you're exceptionally hungry and need to be satiated. On other days, you may only need to pull the lever down halfway. Just know that you do not need to consume every gram of your calculated amount every day to stay in ketosis. Also, more fat does not equal deeper ketosis. Once you are fat adapted, you'll find that you're not as hungry, and you'll pull the fat lever all the way down less frequently. (I wish someone had told me this when I first started keto!)

You want your fats to come from foods such as butter, ghee, avocado oil, coconut oil, full-fat cheese, cream, high-quality meats, nuts, and seeds. When you think of fat, it's important that you train your brain not to imagine donuts and French fries. Fat is not the enemy any longer! Have you ever opened leftover pot roast and pulled out the clumps of fat before reheating your food? Well, those clumps of fat are the exact kinds of fat that we now want to eat!

Protein: The Goal

Ideally protein should come from high-quality meat, seafood, and vegetables. Whenever possible, purchase grass-fed and grass-finished meats, free-range eggs, wild-caught seafood, and organic vegetables. (Fresh and frozen vegetables are better than canned because they have the highest nutrient density.) Believe it or not, broccoli and asparagus and many other vegetables contain protein! In your pre-keto days, you might have tried to amp up your protein by adding beans, legumes, and lentils to your diet. Though those foods are not necessarily *unhealthy*, they are high in carbohydrates and thus not proper for a ketogenic diet. One serving of beans has more than *double* the amount of carbs someone on a ketogenic diet should consume in an entire day.

Remember the key to a ketogenic diet is to eat in a way that puts you in a state of nutritional ketosis. That means we consume a high-fat, *moderate*-protein, low-carbohydrate diet every day. The rule of thumb for protein macros is that they are a goal. You should aim to hit all of your protein grams each day, but if you don't, don't sweat it.

If you're an athlete, you might worry that if you don't eat enough protein, you won't gain muscle. Although protein is essential to muscle building, the amino acid found *in* protein, called leucine, is actually what stimulates muscle growth. When you eat keto and are in nutritional ketosis, your leucine levels actually increase.

Consuming an exorbitant amount of protein is not necessary to build muscle. Eating a moderate amount of protein will not stall your physical fitness. For someone looking to build muscle, the recommended protein intake is 1 gram of protein per pound of body weight. So, if you weigh 150 pounds (68 kg), then 150 grams of protein would be appropriate. However, it's always good practice to consult a professional when experimenting with diet and intense physical training.

Carbohydrates: The Limit

When you are limited to 20 to 30 grams of carbohydrates per day, you have to make the most of them. You want the bulk of your carbohydrates to come from healthy sources such as leafy green vegetables, nuts, or seeds. Even cheese has a small amount of carbs—but also a healthy dose of fat and protein, making it an ideal low-carb food for the keto lifestyle.

Carbs are your expensive item in the macro budget. Too many can make you go in the red (that is, kick you out of ketosis), so it's important that you budget wisely and track your expenses.

Carbohydrates can be tricky to track because it seems as if *everything* contains carbs. There is some validity to that. Many foods, especially processed foods, contain carbs. Your ultimate goal should be to eat as cleanly as you can, avoiding processed foods as much as possible.

The wonderful thing about counting carbohydrates is that you can also take into account dietary fiber. Every gram of fiber can be deducted from your total carbohydrates because fiber does not affect blood glucose levels; therefore, it cannot interrupt your state of nutritional ketosis. This practice is called counting net carbs. It's also important to note the third element of the equation, sugar alcohols. I'll get into this more in depth on page 21, but for now, know that when you are reading nutrition labels and see sugar alcohols listed, you may deduct them as well. Here's the formula:

Net carbs = total carbs - fiber - sugar alcohols

Let's break down the net carbohydrate counts for the most commonly eaten foods on a ketogenic diet:

CARBOHYDRATE COUNTS FOR THE MOST COMMONLY CONSUMED FOODS ON A KETOGENIC DIET

Food	Carbohydrate per 100 g (3.5 oz)	Fiber per 100 g (3.5 oz)	Net carbs per 100 g (3.5 oz)
Asparagus	3.88	2.1	1.78
Broccoli	6.64	2.6	4.04
Brussels sprouts	8.95	3.8	5.15
Butter	0	0	0
Cabbage	5.80	2.5	3.3
Carrots	9.58	2.8	6.78
Cauliflower	4.97	2.0	2.97
Eggplant	5.88	3.0	2.88
Eggs	<1	0	<1
Green beans	6.97	2.7	4.27
Kale	4.42	4.1	0.32
Lettuce, iceberg	2.97	1.2	1.77
Lettuce, romaine	3.29	2.1	1.19
Mushrooms, portobello	3.87	1.3	2.57
Mushrooms, white	3.26	1.0	2.26
Onions	9.34	1.7	7.64
Peppers (green bell)	4.64	1.7	2.94
Radishes	3.40	1.6	1.8
Spaghetti squash	6.91	1.5	5.41
Spinach	3.63	2.2	1.43
Zucchini	3.11	1.0	2.11

Source: USDA Food Composition Database

Even though there's no list of "keto-approved foods," when you follow keto, certain foods are typically off the table. Fruits, vegetables, and grains—including apples, bananas, oranges, corn, potatoes, sweet potatoes, beans, legumes, rice, and wheat products—all have higher carbohydrate counts in one serving than is permitted in an entire day of a keto diet! The "How to Replace High-Carb Foods with Keto-Freindly Foods" chart below lists some of them. You might be surprised to see milk on this chart; that's because milk is high in carbs. One cup (240 ml) of whole milk has almost 12 grams of carbs!

HOW TO REPLACE HIGH-CARB FOODS WITH KETO-FRIENDLY FOODS

High-Carbohydrate Food	Low-Carbohydrate Food
Pasta	Zucchini noodles, spaghetti squash, shirataki (konjac) noodles
Rice	Cauliflower rice
Apples, bananas, oranges	Berries
Potatoes	Cauliflower, broccoli
Mashed potatoes	Mashed cauliflower
Milk and soy milk	Unsweetened almond milk and cashew milk
Pizza	Fat head pizza
Bread	Lettuce wraps, low-carb tortillas
Chips	Pork rinds, cheese whisps, such as those made by Cello
Candy bars	Chocolate sweetened with stevia or monk fruit
Peanuts	Macadamia nuts or almonds
All-purpose and whole wheat flour	Almond flour, coconut flour, hazelnut flour
Sugar	Stevia, xylitol, erythritol, monk fruit
Cornstarch	Arrowroot powder or xanthan gum

BONUS RECIPES

Along with the 100 Instant Pot recipes in this cookbook, I thought it might be helpful to include a few keto-friendly recipes that make great accompaniments to some of the delicious meals you are soon to make. These recipes are not for the Instant Pot, but they're very simple, very quick, and can be made while your dish is cooking in the Instant Pot.

FAT HEAD DOUGH

SERVES 4

PREP TIME: 10M

COOK TIME: 10M

TOTAL TIME: 20M

1½ cups (180 g) shredded mozzarella cheese

1 cup (112 g) almond flour

1½ teaspoons baking powder

¼ teaspoon xanthan gum

¼ teaspoon salt

1 egg, beaten

This type of dough is often referred to as "fat head" dough, as the concept was invented by the creators of the documentary *Fat Head*. I played in the kitchen until I found a method that produced a chewy and pillowy bread. It might seem odd to make "bread" dough out of mozzarella cheese, but trust me when I say you're going to love this! With a little creativity, you can transform this basic dough into pizza crust, sandwich thins, or even cinnamon rolls!

Heat the oven to 425°F (220°C, or gas mark 7). Line a baking sheet with parchment paper.

In a microwave-safe bowl, add the mozzarella cheese. Heat in 30-second intervals, stirring between each one, until the cheese is very melty and stretchy.

Add the almond flour, baking powder, xanthan gum, and salt to the cheese. Fold into the cheese with a wooden spoon. Once the almond flour is completely incorporated, add the egg and mix with the wooden spoon until a dough is formed.

Turn the dough out onto a piece of parchment paper. Wet your hands with water and knead the dough until it is uniform in color. You should not see white or yellow spots throughout. Continue wetting your hands, as needed, to prevent sticking. The more you knead the dough, the easier it becomes to manipulate.

Cut the dough into four equal parts. Roll the dough out on the parchment paper to your desired thickness and shape (round for sandwich thins, long for breadsticks, etc.). Transfer to the prepared baking sheet.

Bake until the tops are golden brown, 10 to 15 minutes.

Note: If desired, brush the tops of the dough with melted butter and sprinkle with garlic powder, salt, Parmesan cheese, or ranch seasoning before baking for extra flair!

MACRONUTRIENTS:

Calories: 308	Carbs: 7.9 g	Protein: 16.9 g
Fat: 24.6 g	Fiber: 3.9 g	Net Carbs: 4 g

HOMEMADE EGG NOODLES

SERVES 2

PREP TIME: 5M

COOK TIME: 5M

TOTAL TIME: 10M

4 eggs

2 ounces (56 g) cream cheese, softened

¼ teaspoon xanthan gum

¼ teaspoon salt

Many of the dishes in this book are traditionally served with some sort of pasta. Unfortunately, there are not many keto-friendly pasta options aside from spiraled vegetables. While those are delicious, they're not always in season or practical. These easy-peasy egg noodles are a tasty way to bulk up a dish and sop up your sauce!

Heat the oven to 350°F (180°C, or gas mark 4). Line an 18" x 13" (46 x 33 cm) baking sheet with parchment paper.

Add the eggs, cream cheese, xanthan gum, and salt to a blender or food processor and pulse until completely blended. The mixture will become thick.

Pour the egg mixture onto the baking sheet and use an offset spatula to spread it in an even and thin layer.

Bake until the mixture is set, about 5 minutes.

Remove the sheet from the oven and use a pizza cutter to cut into ribbons of your desired length and width.

Note: You may use a 9" x 13" (23 x 33 cm) baking pan instead of a baking sheet to get thicker noodles.

MACRONUTRIENTS:

Calories: 250	Carbs: 3.5 g	Protein: 14.6 g
Fat: 18.5 g	Fiber: 1.8 g	Net Carbs: 1.7 g

MEXICAN CAULIFLOWER RICE

SERVES 4

PREP TIME: 5M

COOK TIME: 12M

TOTAL TIME: 17M

1 tablespoon (14 g) butter

1 package (12 ounces, or 340 g) frozen cauliflower rice with veggies

7 ounces (about ½ can, or 196 g) diced tomatoes with green chiles

1 packet Sazón Goya seasoning

Pinch salt

¼ cup (60 ml) chicken broth

Chopped cilantro, for garnish (optional)

Mexican food is one of my guilty pleasures, and Spanish rice has long been a preferred side dish for all of my favorite Mexican dishes. I remember the first time I went to our local Mexican joint and didn't eat the rice—I nearly cried. That's when I went home and created this cauliflower rice version. You don't make this in the Instant Pot, but it's very simple to make on the stovetop. Make sure not to skip the Sazón seasoning. You can find it in almost every grocery store in the ethnic foods aisle.

In a large nonstick skillet, melt the butter over medium heat.

Stir in the cauliflower rice and let it cook until it begins to soften, 5 to 6 minutes.

Add the tomatoes, Sazón, and salt and stir to combine. Let the mixture cook for 1 to 2 minutes.

Add the chicken broth and stir. Decrease the heat to medium-low and simmer until all the broth is absorbed, about 5 minutes.

Fluff with a fork and garnish with fresh cilantro, if desired.

MACRONUTRIENTS:

| Calories: 59 | Carbs: 6.6 g | Protein: 2.6 g |
| Fat: 2.8 g | Fiber: 2.3 g | Net Carbs: 4.3 g |

KETO SWEETENERS

Last, but certainly not least, avoid ALL added sugar! This includes honey, agave, pure maple syrup, molasses, granulated sugar, powdered sugar, and brown sugar. You can replace them with sweeteners that are known not to raise blood glucose or insulin levels, such as stevia, erythritol, xylitol, and monk fruit.

Erythritol and xylitol are sugar alcohols that have little to no effect on blood glucose and insulin levels. Though they're called sugar *alcohols*, they don't actually contain any alcohol. In fact, they're derived naturally from many foods we eat. They're perfectly safe and FDA approved for adults and children to consume. Some people notice a cool aftertaste when using erythritol for the first time; it's appropriately called "the cooling effect." You may not notice the aftertaste at all, but if you do, give it time and you'll hardly taste a difference.

My recipes will always call for granulated or powdered erythritol. I choose to work with this sweetener because it yields the most natural tasting product and is an easy 1:1 conversion for sugar. If you prefer monk fruit, xylitol, or another sweetener, read the packaging to see whether any measurement adjustments need to be made before using them.

Stevia and monk fruit are also naturally occurring sweeteners that do not affect blood glucose levels. Stevia comes from the stevia leaf plant. You can purchase it in granulated or liquid form. Some people love stevia, but others find it to be bitter. (I am in the latter group.) Granulated monk fruit is also a fabulous sweetener, but be aware when using it for baking and cooking that the conversion is not always equivalent to sugar in a 1:1 ratio. The package, however, should indicate the proper ratio to use.

You will also see "brown sugar substitute" listed in many recipes. You want to buy one that is erythritol based and not a "brown sugar blend." (It's good practice to always be mindful of the ingredients list when shopping for groceries.)

Even though artificial sweeteners such as aspartame and sucralose do not trigger an insulin response in most people, they should be consumed in small quantities, if at all. Remember that the goal of a ketogenic diet is to eat whole, clean, real foods as much as possible. If you can't live in a world without Diet Coke, and I am right there with you, just try to limit the amount you consume. You'll find that the less you consume artificial sweeteners, the less you will crave them and enjoy the taste. Thankfully, there are many products on the market these days to make enjoying keto sweets possible—and easy.

KETO + KIDS

When it comes to feeding our children, I adopt an 80/20 approach: 80 percent of the time the kids eat low carb, sugar free, and grain free, and 20 percent of the time they eat like regular kids. I'm fortunate that our children do not suffer from food allergies, so I do not have to plan around that. Our kids eat all of the same main meals that my husband and I do. I am not a short-order cook and refuse to make separate meals for everyone!

I'd be lying if I said their transition to a mostly low-carb diet was an easy one. I heard plenty of griping, witnessed many eye rolls, and watched my kids nearly fake their own deaths to avoid eating vegetables. But you know what? After a little time, they realized I wasn't budging, and they quit resisting me. Their burgers and hot dogs are bunless, just like ours. Their ketchup is sugar free, and their vegetables are not starchy, except for the occasional French fry.

For their snacks, I am more forgiving. I allow them to have fruit, yogurt, and clean granola bars, but I really limit the amount of added sugar they eat. I watch labels closely and buy the best options available. I budget in a way that I can afford high-quality snack items for them. I try to avoid empty carbs such as crackers, bread, or chips because it just leaves them hungry again twenty minutes later. Special occasions such as vacations, birthday parties, or sleepovers are times when I bend the rules.

Of course, every child is different, and what works for my family may not work for yours. Also what works for one sibling might not work for another, either. My children are a great example of that. One child will eat almost anything I give her, but the other would rather go to bed hungry than eat broccoli. The baby, well, she isn't old enough to eat solid food yet, but I have high hopes she'll be my keto kid!

I feel going keto was the best decision for my kids. Take my seven-year-old's most recent checkup: While her height skyrocketed in the previous year, she hadn't gained any weight and her BMI dropped considerably. I mentioned to her pediatrician that we had reduced grains, starches, and sugar, and the doctor said, "Well, whatever you're doing is working. Keep it up!" That reinforced my belief that a low-carb diet is good for children too! Of course, you should consult your pediatrician before making any significant changes to your child's diet, but you can rest assured that eliminating refined sugar and grains from their diet is going to affect them positively.

Even if you decide not to feed your kids keto—and bless your heart for doing all that extra cooking—know that children are sponges and absorb a plethora of information and healthy habits just by observing us. (No pressure, right?) At the very least, it *is* possible to wean your kids from junky foods. If we teach our kids *how* to make healthy choices from a young age, they'll be better equipped to do it on their own when they reach adulthood.

LET'S GO SHOPPING

Now that you've completed a crash course on keto, it's time to dive in and stock your kitchen!

All of the recipes in this cookbook use basic keto-friendly ingredients. This means you won't have to search online to buy *one* special ingredient that you'll use in only one dish. The short list opposite might include something you're not familiar with, but as you work your way through the recipes in this book, you'll see that they are quintessential in a ketogenic kitchen. If you can't find something at your local store, all of these are available to order from online retailers or directly from the brands themselves.

These are a few staple ingredients that you'll want to have before you get cooking:

- Almond flour
- Arrowroot powder ("keto cornstarch")
- Avocado oil
- Brown sugar substitute (for sauces, glazes, and baking)
- Coconut oil or ghee
- Erythritol (granulated and powdered)
- Xanthan gum (for thickening and leavening)

While we're stocking our kitchen, let's talk about a few kitchen tools that will come in handy as you make the recipes in this book:

- 6-quart (5.4 L) Instant Pot
- Instant Pot accessories (covered in chapter 2, page 29)
- Spiralizer
- Food processor or strong blender
- Wooden spoons
- Wire whisk
- Kitchen scale

With these pantry staples and a few kitchen tools, you'll be able to successfully cook your way through this book!

KETO ON A BUDGET

As a mom to three children, I understand the gravity of living within a budget. Our family's biggest budget buster is the grocery store! I'm sure most of you can relate. The rising cost of food, especially organic and all-natural foods, can make even the savviest of shoppers blow a grocery budget without batting an eye!

As I've navigated cooking and shopping for a keto family for a while, I've learned a few things that I can pass along to you:

1. **Plan your meals.** This is my biggest piece of advice in this whole chapter. There's a saying: "Plan ahead or plan to fail." I don't know who coined that phrase, but it is so true! Whether we're talking about your fitness and health goals or your grocery list, planning ahead is key. It only takes a few minutes to sit down and hammer out a three- or four-day meal plan. Not only will it help your budget, but you'll also be more likely to stay committed to your diet when you are prepared.

2. **Plan your menu around the sale items for the week.** I used to try menu planning for two weeks at a time, but I found we wasted too much food that way. Instead, I like to plan out three or four days' worth of meals that coincide with the sales. Plus, I am more likely to stick to my meal plan if I don't feel like I have to commit for such a long period of time.

3. **Always go to the store with a list.** If you don't have a set grocery list, you're more likely to aimlessly wander the store adding unnecessary, and often junky, items to your cart.

4. **Check the manager's special area of the store for discounted meat.** I can typically find good deals on meat to stock my freezer with. Most stores tell you

which days they do reductions, so you are sure not to miss out.

5. **Shop at warehouses for items you use most frequently.** I buy almond flour, organic chicken, organic ground beef, and fresh and frozen vegetables at our warehouse store because the price per ounce or pound is so much less than at the local grocer. It costs a little more upfront, but the savings over a month is priceless!

6. **Don't be afraid to buy store-brand products.** They're typically just as good, sometimes better, than the name-brand items! Do be prudent when comparing the ingredients lists, though, and watch for any low-quality additives.

7. **Beware of the specialty and novelty items.** With the huge surge in popularity around keto, companies are popping up everywhere with new "keto" products. Be it protein bars, candies, special meat sticks, or protein powders, it is inevitable that you will be targeted by all of them. These specialty or novelty items are the fastest way to bust your budget. I do have a few favorites that I build into my monthly budget, but $2 protein bars can add up quickly!

WHAT A FULL DAY OF EATING KETO LOOKS LIKE

I'm a visual learner, so I love maps, charts, spreadsheets, and numbers. Here I've built a few sample meal plans to show you what a full day of eating keto might look like using only recipes in this book. These meal plans are for illustration purposes only, and you will need to use a fitness tracker to create a meal plan that is specific to your macros. However, for reference, these can be used as a general guide to plan your day.

EXAMPLE 1: LOWER-CALORIE DAY

Calories: 1307 Fat: 96 g Protein: 86 g Net Carbs: 15 g				
Breakfast:	**Lunch:**	**Dinner:**	**Dessert:**	**Notes:**
Broccoli-Cheddar Egg Bites	Buffalo Chicken Meatballs (4)	Kentucky Hot Brown Casserole	Double Chocolate Chip Brownie	Use the extra macros to enjoy snacks like cheese, olives, or coffee.

EXAMPLE 2: MODERATE-CALORIE DAY

Calories: 1553 Fat: 119 g Protein: 85 g Net Carbs: 17 g				
Breakfast:	**Lunch:**	**Dinner:**	**Dessert:**	**Notes:**
Cinnamon Roll Coffee Cake	Chili-Lime Turkey Burger with Sriracha-Lime Dipping Sauce	Deconstructed Egg Rolls with Peanut Sauce	Salted Caramel Pumpkin Cheesecake	A day like this contains ample fat and protein to sustain you all day.

EXAMPLE 3: HIGHER-PROTEIN DAY

Calories: 1354 Fat: 86 g Protein: 102 g Net Carbs: 24 g				
Breakfast:	**Lunch:**	**Dinner:**	**Dessert:**	**Notes:**
Asparagus and Gruyère Frittata	Chicken Zoodle Soup	Maple-Bourbon Salmon, Faux Mac and Cheese, and Southern-Style Green Beans	Crème Brûlée	A day like this contains ample fat and protein to sustain you all day.

EXAMPLE 4: NEARLY ZERO-CARB DAY

Calories: 1117 Fat: 86 g Protein: 71 g Net Carbs: 8 g				
Breakfast:	**Lunch:**	**Dinner:**	**Dessert:**	**Notes:**
Baked Pizza Eggs	Un-Sloppy Joes	Cod Fillets with Basil Butter and Broccoli with Garlic-Herb Cheese Sauce	Crème Brûlée	Add fat and protein to your day without increasing carbs by eating olives or salami with cream cheese; pickles are also a good zero-carb option.

CHAPTER 2

Get to Know Your Instant Pot

Whether your Instant Pot is still sitting in the box, collecting dust in a closet, or displayed proudly on your countertop, this chapter is going to teach you all the things you need to know to successfully cook your way through this cookbook.

The Instant Pot has risen in popularity since its debut in 2010, becoming one of the most purchased and gifted kitchen items for Christmas in 2017. The ease of use, speedy cooking times, and ability to cook foods from frozen are just a sample of the numerous appealing characteristics of the Instant Pot. In other words, it's for everybody!

The Instant Pot allows you to cook a meal from start to finish in a fraction of the time it would take on the stove, in the oven, or in a slow cooker, without compromising the integrity of the food. You can sauté, steam, slow cook, and pressure cook all in the same pot—and the food tastes as if it's been simmering all day. Fixing an entire supper in one pot gives you more time to enjoy your meal and your company, and less time cleaning up the kitchen.

Perhaps the most well-known feature of the Instant Pot is its pressure cooker function. Pressure cookers have been around for ages, but most people still imagine the old 1950s-style stovetop pressure cookers that they've seen sitting in their grandma's cabinet. Long gone are the days of singed eyebrows, busted ceilings, and exploding pots. The Instant Pot has revolutionized pressure cooking for the modern-day home cook.

Its built-in safety features are like insurance for you and your home. All Instant Pots come with locking lids, anti-block shields (to prevent blockages in the steam release pipe), automatic temperature control, burn protection, electrical and thermal fuses, and automatic pressure control. You can rest assured that your Instant Pot is not going to accidentally blow a hole through your ceiling!

For those who wonder how an Instant Pot is any better than stovetop cooking or slow cooking, I have this to say:

No added heat in the kitchen!

No babysitting the stove or oven!

It travels easily, allowing you to fix virtually anything anywhere! (I'm looking at you, campgrounds and road trips.)

FUNCTIONALITY

Instant Pot currently manufactures nine different models of pressure cookers. All of the models are relatively similar, but a few come with special functions, such as Bluetooth or Wi-Fi. For the purposes of this book, I'll be using the Duo Plus 6-quart (5.7 L) model.

Though the high-tech functions are not necessary to make the recipes in this book, size is important. Obviously, a smaller pot is going to hold less food than a larger pot. Also, different-size pots require different cook times because each pot takes different amounts of time to reach pressure. Last, the larger the pot, the more liquid it will require to get to pressure.

All Instant Pots have a HIGH and LOW pressure setting, so no matter which model you have, you will be able to make *all* the recipes in this book. The only exception to this is if a recipe calls for steaming vegetables using the STEAM setting. This function allows you to steam vegetables quickly without using as much pressure as the HIGH or LOW pressure setting. I give alternative cooking methods in recipes for those Instant Pots without a STEAM setting.

The majority of Instant Pots have preset programs for things such as soup, beans, meat, cake, yogurt, eggs, sauté, and slow cook. These programs have preset times and pressure settings, but they can be manually adjusted to fit a recipe's requirements. The neat thing about these programs is that they store the last-used setting. For example, if you make chili once a week and use the CHILI program set at HIGH pressure for 30 minutes, you only have to set it once, and each time going forward the cook time and pressure will already be set.

When making the recipes in this book, you may opt to use the MANUAL/PRESSURE COOK button or the corresponding function button (that is, cake, soup, meat, etc.). Either way, you'll have to adjust the pressure level and cook times to what is called for in the recipe.

Keep in mind that the cook times listed in the recipes *do not include the time it takes for the pot to come to pressure.* The amount of time it takes for the pot to come to pressure varies greatly depending on the model and size you have, the altitude at which you live, and how full the pot is. A good rule of thumb is to expect an additional 5 to 10 minutes for pressure to be fully reached. Although most recipes require a manual release, which means you depressurize the pot by hand, others require a natural release. A *natural release* means that the pot depressurizes on its own, slowly, which requires additional time.

All Instant Pots also have delayed-start-time and keep-warm options. This last feature is especially helpful if you're preparing other foods while your Instant Pot is in use, you're not going to eat your food as soon as it's ready, or you're entertaining guests and want to keep your food warm.

ACCESSORIES FOR YOUR INSTANT POT

There are few accessories you will need to make the majority of the recipes in this book. All of them can be purchased online very inexpensively. I guarantee they will not be a one-and-done purchase!

Trivet

Every Instant Pot includes a trivet. This is essentially a shelf that goes inside the inner pot. You may see it called a *steam rack* as well. You will use the trivet any time you are cooking something that needs to be elevated from the liquid at the bottom of the pot.

7" (18 cm)/1.5-quart (1.4 L) Baking Dish

A round baking dish is essential for Instant Pot cooking. A baking dish allows you to make casseroles, cakes, or any kind of dish that you do not want to come into contact with liquid. I recommend something porcelain, similar to CorningWare.

7" (18 cm) Bundt Pan and Springform Pan

A small round Bundt pan and springform pan are essential to making cakes and cheesecakes. There are several brands available that make items specifically to fit in your Instant Pot.

Egg Mold

An egg mold is a round silicone tray with cavities for cooking individual items such as the Two-Bite Pancakes (page 38) and Broccoli-Cheddar Egg Bites (page 41). They come with a lid for easy storage and may also be used in the oven and microwave.

Steamer Basket

A steamer basket is used for making hard-boiled eggs, steaming vegetables, and cooking seafood. I prefer a steamer basket with a silicone handle for safe and easy removal of the basket from the pot.

Extra Sealing Ring

I highly recommend purchasing an extra sealing ring. I learned the hard way that the sealing ring, which is a rubber or silicone piece that fits inside the lid, absorbs the flavors and smells of whatever you've cooked. If you're making a pot of chili followed by a chocolate cake, there is a good chance that cake might have the slightest hint of chili. Having a *savory* sealing ring and a *sweet* sealing ring is an inexpensive and wise purchase.

Additional Inner Pot and Glass Lid

If you plan to use your Instant Pot frequently, I suggest purchasing a second inner pot and glass lid. This will allow you to cook multiple times without needing to transfer food to storage containers and then wash and reuse the inner pot each time. They're not an expensive addition and can really maximize the potential use of your Instant Pot.

CARING FOR YOUR INSTANT POT

Perhaps one of the qualities I love most about the Instant Pot is that it requires minimal care. Nothing can diminish the excitement of a new kitchen appliance like one that is high maintenance. Thankfully, the Instant Pot is a low-maintenance gal.

All of the pieces that touch food in the Instant Pot can be washed in the dishwasher. This includes the sealing ring, inner pot, trivet, and other accessories. You can even put the lid in the dishwasher if you really need to. The cooker base and heating element should never be submerged in water, but they do not come into contact with food, so theoretically they should not get dirty.

If the outside of your Instant Pot gets dirty, it may be wiped off with a damp cloth. I also recommend using a cheap child's toothbrush to clean the part of the cook base that the lid locks into. You'll find that as you use your Instant Pot often, food particles magically find their way underneath the locking portion of the lid. How that happens, I have yet to figure out, but it caused quite the conundrum the first time I attempted to clean it. Using a dry toothbrush will allow you to brush any crumbs or pieces of food out from underneath the edges of the cook base.

My last bit of advice pertains to burnt-on foods. At some point in your Instant Pot cooking career, you will get a thick layer of burnt food on the bottom of your inner pot. It truly is inevitable. In that event, you will panic, thinking that you've destroyed the pot and nothing will ever cook properly again. Let me assure you, that is not the case! Remember that STEAM setting I mentioned earlier? If you have burnt-on food, simply add 1 cup (240 ml) of water to your pot, close the lid, and cook on STEAM mode for 1 to 2 minutes. When it's complete and you open the pot, all of that burnt-on food will peel right off the pot. Essentially, you're deglazing the pot with water and steam—genius!

Now you're ready to get cooking (and eating)! Which recipes are you going to make first?! May I suggest the Crème Brûlèe (page 180) or Red Wine Beef Stew (page 74)?

CHAPTER 3

Breaking Your Fast

Is it just me, or does breakfast food taste better after you've been awake for a few hours? I think breakfast foods should be celebrated during all hours of the day! In fact, if you intermittent fast, your first meal (when you break your fast) may be later in the afternoon or evening. Whenever you choose to break your fast, these sweet and savory recipes are sure to please. Each of these recipes is meal-prep friendly, too, so you can be well fed as your start your day!

NO-PEEL HARD-BOILED EGGS

SERVES 6

PREP TIME: 5M

COOK TIME: 3M

TOTAL TIME: 8M

½ cup (120 ml) water

6 eggs

ACCESSORIES NEEDED:

Trivet

Silicone muffin cup liners

Eggs are one of the best foods you can eat on a ketogenic diet. They're full of healthy fat, cholesterol, and protein! Use your hard-boiled eggs for a ready-made breakfast, to make egg salad or deviled eggs, or as a grab-and-go snack option throughout the week. Making hard-boiled eggs is one of my favorite uses of my Instant Pot because they always come out absolutely perfect. Any trick that takes over the babysitting duties stovetop eggs require is a winner in my book!

Place the trivet in the pot and add the water.

Crack each egg into a silicone cup. Carefully place the cups on top of the trivet.

Close the lid and seal the vent. Cook on HIGH pressure for 3 minutes for soft-boiled eggs and 5 minutes for hard-boiled eggs. Quick release the steam.

Carefully remove the cups from the pot. Use a spoon to pop the eggs out of the cups. Store in an airtight container in the refrigerator for up to one week.

Note: If you want the eggs in traditional hard-boiled shape, do not crack them into the muffin cup liners. Instead, place the eggs in the steamer basket and follow the same instructions. You can cook a dozen eggs at a time by using the steamer basket method!

MACRONUTRIENTS:

Calories: 178	Carbs: 0.8 g	Protein: 31.7 g
Fat: 4.3 g	Fiber: 0.1 g	Net Carbs: 0.7 g

1-MINUTE BREAKFAST STEAK

SERVES 2

PREP TIME: 5M

COOK TIME: 1M

TOTAL TIME: 6M

½ cup (120 ml) water

1 pound (454 g) boneless beef sirloin steak

½ teaspoon + 1 pinch salt

½ teaspoon black pepper

2 tablespoons (28 g) butter, softened

1 clove garlic, minced

¼ teaspoon dried parsley

¼ teaspoon dried rosemary

Pinch of dried thyme

ACCESSORY NEEDED:

Trivet

Steak and eggs are one of my favorite breakfast meals. Frying up steak takes a little more time than I typically have on a busy morning, so I eliminated the frying pan and substituted the Instant Pot. The pressure tenderizes leaner (and cheaper) cuts of beef quickly and perfectly. Add a little herbed butter for some flavor and fat. Now you can have steak (and eggs) every day of the week!

Add the water to the pot and place the trivet inside.

Season both sides of the steak with the ½ teaspoon salt and the pepper. Place the steak on top of the trivet.

In a small dish, mix the butter, garlic, parsley, rosemary, thyme, and pinch of salt. Add half of the herbed butter to the top of the steak.

Close the lid and seal the vent. Cook on LOW pressure for 1 minute. Quick release the steam.

Remove the steak from the pot. Top with the remaining herbed butter.

Note: If desired, place the steak in a hot skillet or under the broiler to crisp up the edges.

MACRONUTRIENTS:

| Calories: 427 | Carbs: 0.6 g | Protein: 46.7 g |
| Fat: 25.2 g | Fiber: 0.1 g | Net Carbs: 0.5 g |

ASPARAGUS AND GRUYÈRE FRITTATA

SERVES 6

PREP TIME: 10M

COOK TIME: 22M

TOTAL TIME: 37M

6 eggs

6 tablespoons (90 ml) heavy cream

½ teaspoon salt

½ teaspoon black pepper

1 clove garlic, minced

2½ ounces (70 g) chopped asparagus (about 1 cup)

1 tablespoon (14 g) butter

3 ounces (84 g) shredded Gruyère cheese (about 1¼ cups), divided

Cooking spray

3 ounces (84 g) halved cherry tomatoes (optional)

½ cup (120 ml) water

ACCESSORIES NEEDED:

7" (18 cm) baking dish

Trivet

I discovered my love for frittatas as a newlywed. Trying to impress my new husband, I taught myself how to make "fancy eggs." After all, the way to a man's heart is through his stomach, so my momma says. This easy frittata is impressive enough for a brunch and easy enough for meal prep. You can even play around with the cheeses and veggies!

In a large mixing bowl, whisk together the eggs, cream, salt, and pepper. Be careful to whisk long enough so that there are not any pieces of egg white floating through the mixture.

Turn the pot to SAUTÉ mode. Once hot, sauté the asparagus and garlic in the butter until fragrant, about 2 minutes. The asparagus should still be crisp. Press CANCEL. Rinse out the inner pot and return it to the base.

Add the garlic and asparagus to the egg mixture. Add 1 cup (68 g) of the cheese and stir to combine.

Grease the baking dish with cooking spray. Layer the tomatoes, if using, in a single layer on the bottom of the dish. Pour the egg mixture on top of the tomatoes and sprinkle with the remaining ¼ cup (14 g) cheese.

Cover the baking dish tightly with aluminum foil and set the dish on top of the trivet. Add the water to the pot and carefully lower the trivet in.

Close the lid and seal the vent. Cook on HIGH pressure for 20 minutes. Quick release the steam.

Remove the dish from the pot and remove the foil. Blot off any excess moisture with a paper towel. Let the frittata cool for 5 to 10 minutes before flipping onto a plate.

Note: To reduce the carbs in this dish, the tomatoes are optional. If you omit them, complete the recipe as directed, simply skipping the tomato step.

MACRONUTRIENTS:

Calories: 205	Carbs: 2.2 g	Protein: 11.2 g
Fat: 16.7 g	Fiber: 0.6 g	Net Carbs: 1.8 g

TWO-BITE PANCAKES

SERVES 6 (3 BITES
EACH)

PREP TIME: 10M

COOK TIME: 45M

TOTAL TIME: 55M

2 cups (224 g) almond
   flour

4 eggs

½ cup (112 g) butter,
   melted

¼ cup (60 ml) + ½ cup
   (120 ml) water, divided

2 tablespoons (25 g)
   granulated erythritol

1 tablespoon (15 ml)
   avocado oil

1 teaspoon vanilla extract

1 teaspoon baking
   powder

Pinch of salt

ACCESSORIES NEEDED:

Egg mold

Trivet

These keto pancakes are the second-most popular recipe on my blog—so popular that I knew I needed to adapt it for the Instant Pot. They are the perfect size for little hands and big hands alike to eat on the go! Whether you're sitting in board meetings or in a classroom, the fat and protein in these Two-Bite Pancakes will keep you full all morning long.

In a blender or food processor, combine the flour, eggs, melted butter, ¼ cup (60 ml) of the water, erythritol, avocado oil, vanilla, baking powder, and salt. Pulse until fully combined and smooth. Let the batter rest for 5 minutes before cooking.

Fill each cup with 2 tablespoons (30 ml) of batter, about two-thirds of the way full. Cover the mold with aluminum foil and place on the trivet.

Add the remaining ½ cup (120 ml) water to the pot. Place the trivet in the pot.

Close the lid and seal the vent. Cook on HIGH pressure for 15 minutes. Quick release the steam.

Repeat with the remaining batter, until all the batter is used. Add more water to the pot before cooking each batch, if needed.

Note: These reheat very well. Make them ahead of time and freeze or refrigerate for a meal prep breakfast option. Reheat in the microwave and dip them in your favorite sugar-free maple syrup.

MACRONUTRIENTS:

| Calories: 424 | Carbs: 8.3 g | Protein: 12.2 g |
| Fat: 38.8 g | Fiber: 4 g | Net Carbs: 4.3 g |

BAKED PIZZA EGGS

SERVES 1

PREP TIME: 5M

COOK TIME: 10M

TOTAL TIME: 20M

1 tablespoon (14 g) butter, cut into small pieces

2 tablespoons (30 g) low-carb marinara sauce

3 eggs

2 tablespoons (10 g) grated Parmesan cheese

¼ teaspoon Italian seasoning

1 cup (240 ml) water

ACCESSORIES NEEDED:

Small oven-safe bowl or large ramekin

Trivet

Cold pizza for breakfast is delicious, but because pizza isn't keto friendly, we go with the next best thing: pizza eggs. This little bowl of eggs is a great way to jump-start the day. The high fat content will keep you satiated for hours, and the protein will give you energy. You could even dip some low-carb toast or grilled Fat Head Dough (page 18) in it for the full pizza effect. Switch up the toppings to personalize your eggs. The world is your oyster, er, egg!

Place the butter pieces on the bottom of the oven-safe bowl. Scatter the marinara sauce on top of the butter. Do not worry about it being perfectly even.

Crack the eggs on top of the marinara sauce. Sprinkle the cheese and Italian seasoning on top.

Cover the bowl with aluminum foil. Add the water to the pot. Place the bowl on the trivet and carefully lower it into the pot.

Close the lid and seal the vent. Cook on LOW pressure for 10 minutes. Quick release the steam.

Let the eggs rest for 5 minutes before eating.

MACRONUTRIENTS:

| Calories: 376 | Carbs: 2.4 g | Protein: 22.9 g |
| Fat: 29.7 g | Fiber: 0.3 g | Net Carbs: 2.1 g |

BROCCOLI-CHEDDAR EGG BITES

SERVES 7

PREP TIME: 10M

COOK TIME: 15M

TOTAL TIME: 25M

5 eggs

3 tablespoons (45 ml) heavy cream

⅛ teaspoon salt

⅛ teaspoon black pepper

1 ounce (28 g) finely chopped broccoli

1 ounce (28 g) shredded Cheddar cheese

½ cup (120 ml) water

ACCESSORIES NEEDED:

Egg mold (7)

Trivet

Soft egg bites have become a very popular breakfast item at coffee shops, but they come with a hefty price tag! Your Instant Pot is the perfect vessel to re-create the trendy menu item at a fraction of the cost. These little egg bites are also great for kids running to catch the school bus or while you make your morning commute.

Crack the eggs into a blender or food processor. Add the cream, salt, and pepper and pulse until smooth.

Evenly distribute the broccoli among the egg cups.

Pour the egg mixture on top of the broccoli, filling the cups about three-fourths of the way full.

Sprinkle the cheese on top of each cup.

Cover the egg mold tightly with aluminum foil. Add the water to the pot. Place the egg mold on top of the trivet and lower into the pot.

Close the lid and seal the vent. Cook on HIGH pressure for 10 minutes. Let the steam naturally release for 5 minutes before manually releasing.

Note: Be sure to measure your ingredients precisely. Too much filling will cause everything to sink to the bottom of the egg. If you have two egg molds, you can double the recipe and stack the containers on top of each other in the pot.

MACRONUTRIENTS:

Calories: 90	Carbs: 0.8 g	Protein: 5.7 g
Fat: 7.1 g	Fiber: 0.1 g	Net Carbs: 0.6 g

CINNAMON ROLL COFFEE CAKE

SERVES 8

PREP TIME: 10M

COOK TIME: 45M

TOTAL TIME: 55M +
    COOLING

My husband is a huge fan of coffee cake, so I had to make one for this book! That's love, right? Well, it sure was love at first bite when he tried this cake. He immediately said, "That would be great with a cup of coffee," which is why this recipe is in the breakfast chapter!

FOR CAKE:

2 cups (224 g) almond flour

1 cup (200 g) granulated erythritol

1 teaspoon baking powder

Pinch of salt

½ cup (120 g) sour cream

2 eggs

4 tablespoons (56 g) butter, melted

2 teaspoons vanilla extract

2 tablespoons (32 g) brown sugar substitute

1½ teaspoons ground cinnamon

Cooking spray

½ cup (120 ml) water

FOR ICING:

2 ounces (56 g) cream cheese, softened

1 cup (192 g) powdered erythritol

1 tablespoon (15 ml) heavy cream

½ teaspoon vanilla extract

ACCESSORIES NEEDED:

7" (18 cm) Bundt pan

Trivet

To make the cake: In the bowl of a stand mixer (or in a bowl with a hand mixer), combine the almond flour, granulated erythritol, baking powder, and salt until no lumps remain.

Add the sour cream, eggs, butter, and vanilla and mix until well combined.

In a separate bowl, mix together the brown sugar substitute and cinnamon.

Grease the Bundt pan with cooking spray. Pour in the cake batter and use a knife to make sure it is level around the pan.

Sprinkle the cinnamon mixture on top and use your knife to swirl it into the batter.

Cover the pan tightly with aluminum foil. Add the water to the pot. Place the Bundt pan on top of the trivet and carefully lower it into the pot.

Close the lid and seal the vent. Cook on HIGH pressure for 45 minutes. Quick release the steam.

Remove the cake from the pot and remove the foil. Blot off any moisture on top of the cake with a paper towel, if necessary.

While the cake is cooling, make the icing: In a small bowl, use a mixer to whip the cream cheese until it is light and fluffy. Slowly add the powdered erythritol and mix until well combined. Add the cream and vanilla and mix until thoroughly combined.

When the cake is cooled, flip it onto a platter and drizzle the icing all over.

MACRONUTRIENTS:

Calories: 314	Carbs: 6.9 g	Protein: 8.6 g
Fat: 27.1 g	Fiber: 3.2 g	Net Carbs: 3.6 g

CHAPTER 4

Appetizers and Party Snacks

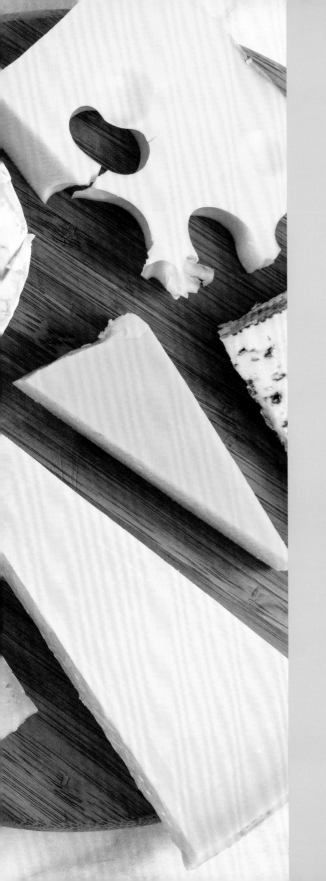

I am not someone who needs a holiday to throw a good party! Entertaining, cooking, and hosting my friends and family is my love language. Whether we're rooting on our favorite football team (Go, VOLS!) or just spending an evening together, these recipes are always a hit. Plus who doesn't love to eat leftover snacks for lunch the next day? Lose the slow cookers and free up space on your counter for more food at your next party—the Instant Pot is the real M.V.P.!

BUFFALO CHICKEN MEATBALLS

YIELD: 20 MEATBALLS

PREP TIME: 25M

COOK TIME: 10M

TOTAL TIME: 35M

1 pound (454 g) ground chicken

1 rib celery, finely diced

1 scallion, finely diced

1 egg

2 tablespoons (30 ml) + 1 cup (240 ml) buffalo wing sauce, divided

½ teaspoon garlic powder

½ teaspoon salt

Pinch of black pepper

½ cup (120 ml) chicken broth

If you're in the mood for buffalo chicken wings but want to avoid the orange fingers and greasy lips, then these little meatballs are perfect for you—no wet wipes required! Fix them for a crowd and you won't have to worry about wing stains on your furniture. These little meatballs pack a punch, so serve some blue cheese or ranch dressing on the side for dipping.

In a bowl, combine the chicken, celery, scallion, egg, 2 tablespoons (30 ml) of the buffalo wing sauce, garlic powder, salt, and pepper. Stir with a wooden spoon until the mixture is well combined.

Use a medium-size cookie scoop to measure out 20 meatballs and place them on a large plate or baking sheet. Each meatball should weigh about 1 ounce (28 g).

Put the plate of meatballs in the freezer for 15 minutes to flash freeze them. This will help them retain their shape during cooking.

Add the broth and ½ cup (120 ml) of the buffalo wing sauce to the pot. Remove the meatballs from the freezer and place them into the pot.

Close the lid and seal the vent. Cook on HIGH pressure for 10 minutes. Quick release the steam.

Use a slotted spoon to remove the meatballs from the pot and transfer to a serving plate or bowl. Top them with the remaining ½ cup (120 ml) buffalo wing sauce.

If desired, place the meatballs on a baking sheet and put them under the broiler for 3 to 5 minutes for a stickier buffalo coating.

MACRONUTRIENTS PER MEATBALL:

Calories: 39	Carbs: 0.3 g	Protein: 4.8 g
Fat: 2.1 g	Fiber: 0.1 g	Net Carbs: 0.2 g

DEEP-DISH PIZZA DIP

SERVES 10

PREP TIME: 5M

COOK TIME: 10M

TOTAL TIME: 15M

4 ounces (112 g) ricotta
    cheese

4 ounces (112 g) cream
    cheese, softened

¾ cup (180 ml) low-carb
    marinara sauce

18 pepperoni slices

1 cup (115 g) shredded
    mozzarella cheese

1 cup (240 ml) water

ACCESSORIES NEEDED:

7" (18 cm) baking dish

Trivet

Hospitality is my love language. I love to feed people and make them feel welcomed. One time I was hosting a party, and one of my non-keto friends attempted to make keto brownies. They were quite possibly the worst things in the entire world, and the reactions on everyone's faces were priceless. Bless her heart. We still laugh about that night! Thankfully, this keto-friendly pizza dip is so good that all of your friends and family, keto or not, will love it!

In a small bowl, combine the ricotta cheese and cream cheese. Spread it in an even layer in the bottom of the baking dish.

Spread the marinara sauce on top of the cheese mixture.

Layer half of the pepperoni slices on top of the marinara sauce.

Sprinkle the mozzarella cheese on top of the pepperoni layer. Top with the remaining pepperoni.

Add the water to the pot. Cover the baking dish with aluminum foil. Place the dish on the trivet and carefully lower it into the pot.

Close the lid and seal the vent. Cook on HIGH pressure for 10 minutes. Quick release the steam.

If desired, place the baking dish under the broiler, uncovered, to brown the cheese, about 5 minutes.

Note: Serve this pizza dip with squares of Fat Head Dough (page 18), crisped up low-carb tortillas, or your favorite crunchy snack.

MACRONUTRIENTS:

Calories: 121	Carbs: 1.8 g	Protein: 5.9 g
Fat: 10 g	Fiber: 0.2 g	Net Carbs: 1.6 g

GAME DAY MEATBALLS

SERVES 30

   (2 MEATBALLS EACH)

PREP TIME: 3M

COOK TIME: 7M

TOTAL TIME: 15M

¼ cup (60 ml) water

2 packages (14 ounces, or 392 g, each) frozen meatballs (60 meatballs total)

8 ounces (227 g) sugar-free blackberry jam

½ cup (120 ml) sugar-free BBQ sauce

¼ cup (60 ml) sriracha

Meatballs are an essential appetizer for any good party! I ketofied the classic BBQ party meatball recipe by substituting sugar-free jam and BBQ sauce. I added a bit of sriracha to the mix to make them sweet and spicy! These meatballs are a little higher in carbs, so portion control will be important. You can dial down the carbs by omitting the sriracha and using a high-quality sugar-free jam.

Pour the water into the pot and add the meatballs.

In a small bowl, whisk together the jam, BBQ sauce, and sriracha. Pour the sauce over the meatballs.

Close the lid and seal the vent. Cook on HIGH pressure for 7 minutes. Quick release the steam.

Stir the meatballs to make sure they are evenly coated with sauce. Transfer to a serving bowl. Let rest for a few minutes so the sauce thickens up a bit before serving.

MACRONUTRIENTS:

Calories: 75	Carbs: 5.7 g	Protein: 4.7 g
Fat: 4.3 g	Fiber: 1.4 g	Net Carbs: 4.3 g

GARLIC-PARMESAN CHICKEN WINGS

SERVES 4

PREP TIME: 5M

COOK TIME: 13M

TOTAL TIME: 18M

3 pounds (1362 g) chicken wings (drummettes, flats, or whole wings)

2 teaspoons avocado oil

1 tablespoon (5 g) grated Parmesan cheese, divided

½ teaspoon salt, divided

½ teaspoon onion powder, divided

½ teaspoon garlic powder, divided

Pinch of black pepper

½ cup (120 ml) water

1 tablespoon (14 g) butter, melted

ACCESSORY NEEDED:

Steamer basket

Any day is a good day for chicken wings! I love that keto allows me to still eat chicken wings and have zero guilt. These wings are reminiscent of the popular restaurant version but much cleaner and healthier. The Instant Pot cooks these babies in a fraction of the time your oven can and saves you from cleaning up grease splatters! You can make these for a crowd or a quiet night at home.

Heat the broiler.

Place the wings on a large plate or baking sheet. Pat both sides dry with a paper towel. Drizzle the avocado oil on top of the wings and use your hands to coat them evenly.

In a small bowl, mix half the cheese, half the salt, half the onion powder, half the garlic powder, and a pinch of pepper. Toss the wings in the rub.

Place the wings in the steamer basket. Add the water to the pot.

Close the lid and seal the vent. Cook on HIGH pressure for 8 minutes. Quick release the steam.

Use tongs to carefully remove the wings from the basket and place them flat on a clean baking sheet. Broil the wings to crisp up the skins, about 5 minutes.

In a small bowl, combine the remaining cheese and spices with the melted butter. Brush the mixture on top of the wings before serving.

MACRONUTRIENTS FOR THE SAUCE:

Calories: 578	Carbs: 0.5 g	Protein: 0.9 g
Fat: 5.8 g	Fiber: 0.1 g	Net Carbs: 0.4 g

Note: The macronutrients for the chicken wings will vary based on size and the ratio of meat to bones.

MILLIONAIRE CHEESE DIP

SERVES 10

PREP TIME: 5M

COOK TIME: 13M

TOTAL TIME: 18M

2 teaspoons avocado oil

½ pound (227 g) large shrimp, peeled and deveined

1 cup (115 g) shredded Cheddar cheese

8 ounces (227 g) cream cheese, softened

½ cup (112 g) mayonnaise

2 scallions, sliced

3 pieces bacon, cooked and crumbled

½ teaspoon crab boil seasoning

Pinch of salt

Pinch of black pepper

½ cup (120 ml) water

ACCESSORIES NEEDED:

7" (18 cm) baking dish

Trivet

This dip is so decadent, it's fine enough for a millionaire. We call this a "fancy dip" in our house, and I serve it for special occasions. It always makes an appearance on New Year's Eve. This one will definitely be a hit with all of your party guests!

Turn the pot to SAUTÉ mode. Once hot, add the avocado oil and shrimp. Cook until the shrimp are pink and no longer translucent, 2 to 3 minutes. Be careful not to overcook the shrimp. Press CANCEL. Remove them to a plate and set aside to cool. Rinse out the pot and place it back inside the base.

In a small bowl, combine the Cheddar cheese, cream cheese, mayonnaise, scallions, bacon pieces, crab boil seasoning, salt, and pepper. Mix well to make sure all of the ingredients are evenly dispersed.

Coarsely chop the shrimp. Fold into the cheese mixture.

Transfer the dip to the baking dish. Cover with aluminum foil. Place the dish on top of the trivet and carefully lower it into the pot. Add the water to the pot.

Close the lid and seal the vent. Cook on HIGH pressure for 10 minutes. Quick release the steam.

Note: Try lump crab in place of the shrimp. This dip is also really good cold.

MACRONUTRIENTS:

Calories: 287	Carbs: 1.8 g	Protein: 12.5 g
Fat: 25.8 g	Fiber: 0.1 g	Net Carbs: 1.7 g

CHICKEN WING DIP

SERVES 8

PREP TIME: 5M

COOK TIME: 40M

TOTAL TIME: 45M

½ cup (120 ml) water

1½ pounds (680 g) boneless, skinless chicken breasts

1 cup (240 ml) buffalo wing sauce

¼ cup (60 ml) ranch dressing

2 tablespoons (28 g) butter, melted

8 ounces (227 g) cream cheese

ACCESSORY NEEDED:

Trivet

Football season is a big deal in our family. Game-day Saturdays are made for cheering on our team with all the yummy snacks. Chicken wings have always been a favorite, but they're messy and not very kid (or sofa) friendly. This dip provides all the flavors of the bone-in wings without the fuss. Serve it with sliced radishes, celery sticks, or pork rinds for dipping.

Pour the water into the pot and place the trivet inside. Place the chicken on top of the trivet.

Close the lid and seal the vent. Cook on HIGH pressure for 15 minutes. Let the steam naturally release for 10 minutes before manually releasing. Press CANCEL.

Remove the chicken and trivet from the pot. Place the chicken on a cutting board and shred with two forks. Discard the water remaining in the pot. Return the shredded chicken to the pot.

Add the buffalo sauce, ranch dressing, and melted butter and stir to combine. Add the cream cheese on top but do not stir again.

Close the lid and seal the vent. Cook on LOW pressure for 5 minutes. Quick release the steam.

Remove the lid. Stir the chicken until the mixture is well combined.

Note: You may use frozen chicken breasts without adjusting the cook time.

MACRONUTRIENTS:

Calories: 235	Carbs: 1.5 g	Protein: 18.5 g
Fat: 16.8 g	Fiber: 0 g	Net Carbs: 1.5 g

PIMENTO CHEESE DIP

SERVES 8 (¼ CUP,
    OR 58 G, EACH)
PREP TIME: 10M
COOK TIME: 5M
TOTAL TIME: 15M

3 cups (345 g) freshly
    shredded extra-sharp
    Cheddar cheese

2 jars (4 ounces, or 112 g,
    each) diced pimentos,
    drained

½ cup (112 g) mayonnaise

¼ cup (60 ml) heavy
    cream

½ teaspoon
    Worcestershire sauce

½ teaspoon salt

¼ teaspoon onion powder

Pinch of black pepper

1 cup (240 ml) water

ACCESSORIES NEEDED:

7" (18 cm) baking dish

Trivet

Pimento cheese is a staple at all Southern events. Folks eat it on a sandwich, spread it on crackers, or just by the forkful! My Gran always had a jar of it in her fridge when I'd visit as a little girl. While it's great served cold, it's also delicious melted down. I love to serve this to my company with crispy pieces of bacon, sliced radishes, or pork rinds. Bonus: Use the leftover dip for Pimento Cheese Crack Chicken (page 137)!

Add the cheese, pimentos, mayonnaise, cream, Worcestershire sauce, salt, onion powder, and pepper to the baking dish.

Add the water to the pot. Place the baking dish on top of the trivet and carefully lower it into the pot.

Close the lid and seal the vent. Cook on HIGH pressure for 5 minutes. Quick release the steam.

Carefully remove the trivet from the pot. Stir the cheese dip until it is well combined.

Note: Be sure to shred your own cheese for this dish. The dip will be grainy if you use packaged pre-shredded cheese, which comes caked in a powdered starch to keep the shreds from clumping.

MACRONUTRIENTS:

| Calories: 229 | Carbs: 1.5 g | Protein: 7.3 g |
| Fat: 22.5 g | Fiber: 0.5 g | Net Carbs: 1 g |

QUESO FUNDIDO

SERVES 20 (¼ CUP, OR
58 G, EACH)
PREP TIME: 5M
COOK TIME: 10M
TOTAL TIME: 15M

1 pound (454 g) ground
hot sausage or Mexican
chorizo

1 pound (454 g) processed
yellow melting cheese
(such as Velveeta),
cubed

8 ounces (227 g) cream
cheese, cubed

1 can (10 ounces, or 280 g)
diced tomatoes with
green chiles

¾ cup (180 ml) heavy
cream

The Mexican restaurant in our little town has an appetizer called Queso Fundido that I just love. I'm not positive how *they* make it, but I re-created a version at home to share with you. It reminds me of a classic Ro-Tel cheese dip, but a little spicier and a lot more fun. Make this for your next get-together and you'll be the hit of the party! Eat with pork rinds, celery sticks, quesadillas, radish chips, or any of your favorite crunchy snacks.

Turn the pot to SAUTÉ mode. Once hot, add the sausage and cook until no longer pink, 3 to 4 minutes. If your meat produces more than 1 tablespoon (15 ml) of grease, drain off the excess.

In this order, add the yellow cheese, cream cheese, and tomatoes (with juice). This will ensure that the cheese and tomatoes do not scorch terribly on the bottom of the pot. Do *not* stir the mixture.

Close the lid and seal the vent. Cook on LOW pressure for 3 minutes. Quick release the steam.

Open the lid and stir the mixture until all of the cheese is melted and incorporated. There may be a little bit stuck to the bottom, but that is okay. Add the cream and stir to combine.

Note: If you're not serving this right away, you may use the WARM setting to keep the dip hot without cooking. Use the leftovers as a topping for bunless burgers, or whisk it into tomorrow morning's scrambled eggs for a decadent keto-friendly breakfast!

MACRONUTRIENTS:

Calories: 163	Carbs: 2.4 g	Protein: 6.6 g
Fat: 13.3 g	Fiber: 0.1 g ,	Net Carbs: 2.3 g

ZERO-CALORIE SOUTHERN SWEET TEA

YIELD: 2 QUARTS (2 L)

PREP TIME: 0M

COOK TIME: 5M

TOTAL TIME: 5M

2 quarts (2 L) water

5 black tea bags, tags removed

¾ cup (144 g) powdered erythritol

Southerners are known for sweet tea. The sweeter, the better! It gets so hot in the South that many folks used to make tea by letting the bags steep in the water out in the sun instead of on the stove. We call it "sun tea." As fun as it is to keep the tradition alive, I like to make my tea fast so I can drink it sooner! The Instant Pot makes perfectly brewed tea in just 5 minutes. You can have a pitcher on hand at all times with this speedy method.

Add the water to the pot. Place the tea bags inside.

Close the lid and seal the vent. Cook on HIGH pressure for 5 minutes. Quick release the steam.

Add the powdered erythritol to a pitcher and pour the hot tea on top. Stir until the sweetener is dissolved. Serve cold.

Note: For stronger tea, let the steam naturally release for 5 to 10 minutes before manually releasing.

CHAPTER 5

Soups, Stews, and Chilis

P ut me in front of a fireplace with a good book and hot cup of soup and I am one happy girl! This chapter is chock-full of recipes that my family loves, and I know yours will too. One of the best, and probably most celebrated, functions of the Instant Pot is its ability to make soup taste like it's been simmering all day in less time than it takes to run your dishwasher. Soups not only make great welcome-wagon meals, they also freeze and reheat fabulously. Don't wait for cold weather to give one of these a go!

BROCCOLI-CHEDDAR SOUP

YIELD: 10½ CUPS
(2520 ML)

SERVES 7 (1½ CUPS, OR
360 ML, EACH)

PREP TIME: 10M

COOK TIME: 5M

TOTAL TIME: 15M

3 cups (720 ml) chicken
broth

1 pound (454 g) broccoli
florets

8 ounces (227 g) diced
radishes

1½ ounces (42 g) diced
carrot

1½ teaspoons salt

½ teaspoon black pepper

½ teaspoon garlic powder

2 cups (230 g) shredded
Cheddar cheese

½ cup (120 ml) heavy
cream

If you're looking for a way to sneak veggies into your kids' diets, soup is a great option. This Broccoli-Cheddar Soup is creamy, cheesy, and oh so comforting. The radishes add texture, similar to potatoes, and also pack an extra punch of potassium and magnesium (a.k.a. electrolytes). Serve your soup with a big leafy green salad for a simple yet satisfying meal.

Add the chicken broth, broccoli, radishes, carrot, salt, pepper, and garlic powder to the pot.

Close the lid and seal the vent. Cook on HIGH pressure for 5 minutes. Quick release the steam.

Add the cheese to the soup and stir until all the cheese is melted. Add the cream and stir until well combined.

Use an immersion blender to puree the soup until the desired consistency is reached. Alternatively, transfer to a standard blender and blend in batches.

MACRONUTRIENTS:

| Calories: 190 | Carbs: 8.2 g | Protein: 3.9 g |
| Fat: 13.8 g | Fiber: 2.4 g | Net Carbs: 5.8 g |

CINCINNATI-STYLE CHILI

YIELD: 6 CUPS (1440 G)

SERVES 6 (1 CUP, OR
   240 G, EACH)

PREP TIME: 10M

COOK TIME: 24M

TOTAL TIME: 34M

1 tablespoon (15 ml)
   avocado oil

1 pound (454 g) ground
   beef

5 ounces (140 g) chopped
   onion (about 1 cup)

1 clove of garlic, minced

1 tablespoon (7 g)
   unsweetened cocoa
   powder

1 tablespoon (8 g) chili
   powder

1½ teaspoons ground
   cinnamon

1 teaspoon ground
   nutmeg

1 teaspoon ground
   allspice

¼ teaspoon black pepper

¾ teaspoon salt

¼ teaspoon cayenne
   pepper

1 can (14.5 ounces, or
   406 g) diced tomatoes

¼ cup (60 ml) beef broth

2 tablespoons (30 ml)
   Worcestershire sauce

1 tablespoon (15 ml) red
   wine vinegar

Wherever you're from, I'd bet that you have a special way of making chili. It's one of those foods that is unique in every region of our beautiful country. Like most places, Cincinnati is proud of its recipe! Don't be alarmed by the unusual spices. This chili might not be traditional, but it is absolutely delicious! People come from all over to eat a bowl of this distinctive chili. I'm saving you the airfare with this low-carb version of a world-famous treat!

Turn the pot to SAUTÉ mode and add the avocado oil. Once hot, add the ground beef.

Brown the beef, breaking it apart into small pieces with a wooden spoon. When the meat is only slightly pink, 3 to 4 minutes, add the onion and garlic. Continue to sauté until the meat is browned. Press CANCEL.

Add the cocoa powder and spices and stir well to coat the meat. Add the tomatoes (with juice), broth, Worcestershire, and vinegar.

Close the lid and seal the vent. Cook on HIGH pressure for 20 minutes. Quick release the steam.

Note: Serve this chili "Coney Island style" by topping steamed hot dogs with it, shredded Cheddar cheese, yellow mustard, and a little diced white onion.

MACRONUTRIENTS:

Calories: 227	Carbs: 8.1 g	Protein: 15.2 g
Fat: 14.1 g	Fiber: 2.1 g	Net Carbs: 6 g

CAULIFLOWER AND BACON CHOWDER

YIELD: 14 CUPS (3360 ML)

SERVES 7 (2 CUPS, OR
   480 ML, EACH)

PREP TIME: 10M

COOK TIME: 25M

TOTAL TIME: 35M

2 cups (480 ml) chicken
   broth

5 ounces (140 g) diced
   onion (about 1 small
   onion)

8 ounces (227 g) diced
   bacon, uncooked

1 teaspoon salt

½ teaspoon black pepper

1 large head cauliflower
   (about 2 pounds, or
   908 g)

8 ounces (227 g) cream
   cheese, softened and
   cut into small cubes

½ cup (120 ml) heavy
   cream, at room
   temperature

I love creamy soups that warm you up from the inside out! This Cauliflower and Bacon Chowder is so reminiscent of an old potato soup recipe that I used to love. Dare I say this one is better? The cauliflower becomes so tender in the Instant Pot and takes on the texture of potatoes perfectly. Pair this with some keto sausage balls or cornbread for a warm and comforting meal on those cold winter nights.

Pour the chicken broth into the pot. Add the onion, bacon, salt, and pepper. Stir to combine.

Remove the stems and core from the cauliflower but leave the florets in large pieces. Place the large florets in the pot.

Close the lid and seal the vent. Cook on HIGH pressure for 25 minutes. Quick release the steam.

Use a potato masher and gently break apart the cauliflower. It will be very soft. Be careful not to overmash the cauliflower. You want it to be in little pieces that resemble potatoes.

Add the cream cheese to the soup. Use a wooden spoon to stir the soup until all of the cream cheese is melted through. Add the cream and stir to combine.

MACRONUTRIENTS:

| Calories: 328 | Carbs: 9.1 g | Protein: 16.3 g |
| Fat: 24.6 g | Fiber: 2.7 g | Net Carbs: 6.4 g |

CHICKEN ZOODLE SOUP

YIELD: 6 CUPS (1440 ML)

SERVES 6

PREP TIME: 5M

COOK TIME: 30M

TOTAL TIME: 35M

1½ pounds (680 g)
   boneless, skinless
   chicken breasts

3½ ounces (100 g)
   chopped onion

1½ ounces (42 g)
   diced carrot

2 ribs celery, chopped

3 cups (720 ml) chicken
   broth

2 teaspoons salt

1½ teaspoons poultry
   seasoning

½ teaspoon black pepper

10½ ounces (294 g)
   zucchini noodles

Whether you're sick, have been outside sledding in the snow, or missing your momma, chicken noodle soup has a way of healing us from the inside out. This keto-friendly chicken "zoodle" soup is savory and soothing. If you don't have a spiralizer to make zucchini noodles, you can buy pre-spiraled zoodles in the produce section of most grocery stores. If you have any leftover soup, freeze it in resealable plastic bags for freezer stocking.

Add the chicken, onion, carrot, celery, chicken broth, salt, poultry seasoning, and pepper to the pot.

Close the lid and seal the vent. Cook on HIGH pressure for 25 minutes. Quick release the steam. Press CANCEL.

Remove the chicken from the soup and shred with two forks. Return the chicken to the soup.

Add the zucchini noodles to the hot soup and let sit until the noodles are soft, 5 to 10 minutes. If you'd like a softer noodle, you can cook the soup an additional 1 to 2 minutes on LOW pressure.

Note: Frozen chicken breasts may be used without adjusting the cooking time.

MACRONUTRIENTS:

| Calories: 147 | Carbs: 5.2 g | Protein: 26.5 g |
| Fat: 2.3 g | Fiber: 1.3 g | Net Carbs: 3.9 g |

HOMEMADE CREAM OF CHICKEN SOUP

SERVES 1

PREP TIME: 5M

COOK TIME: 10M

TOTAL TIME: 15M

½ cup (120 ml) heavy cream

½ cup (120 ml) chicken broth

3 tablespoons (42 g) butter

¼ teaspoon poultry seasoning

¼ teaspoon salt

Pinch of black pepper

2 ounces (56 g) cream cheese, softened

¾ teaspoon xanthan gum

Condensed cream soups are notorious ingredients in casseroles. They add great flavor and texture to covered dishes, but they come full of unhealthy oils and preservatives. This soup is easy to make and keep on hand in your refrigerator. Make your favorite casserole keto friendly by replacing the standard canned soup with this clean homemade version.

Combine the cream, chicken broth, butter, poultry seasoning, salt, and pepper in the pot.

Turn the pot to SAUTÉ mode and whisk as the ingredients heat up and the butter melts.

Add the cream cheese and continue whisking until it is completely melted and combined. The soup will begin to bubble or foam up.

Add the xanthan gum and continue whisking until a thick consistency is reached, 2 to 3 minutes.

MACRONUTRIENTS:

Calories: 948	Carbs: 7.3 g	Protein: 9.2 g
Fat: 95.4 g	Fiber: 1.8 g	Net Carbs: 5.5 g

CREAMY GREEN CHILE AND CARNITAS CHILI

YIELD: 10 CUPS (2400 G)

SERVES 5 (2 CUPS, OR
    480 G, EACH)

PREP TIME: 5M

COOK TIME: 25M

TOTAL TIME: 30M

2 cups (480 ml) chicken
    broth

1 pound (454 g) Salsa
    Verde Carnitas
    (page 141)

12 ounces (340 g) green
    chile salsa (salsa verde
    will also work)

1 cup (240 ml) heavy
    cream

4 ounces (112 g) cream
    cheese, softened and
    cut into cubes

Just about everyone I know has a recipe for white chicken chili, but have you ever had a green chile–pork chili? If you like spice, then you're in for a real treat with this. It's so simple and uses only five ingredients. Pair it with a piece of Maple Bacon Corn Bread (page 165), and add a dollop of sour cream or some shredded Monterey Jack cheese to top off your bowl for a true Tex-Mex supper!

Pour the broth into the pot. Add the shredded pork and salsa. Stir to combine.

Close the lid and seal the vent. Cook on HIGH pressure for 25 minutes. Quick release the steam. Press CANCEL.

Remove the lid. Add the cream and cream cheese cubes. Stir until all the cheese is melted.

MACRONUTRIENTS:

Calories: 335	Carbs: 8.3 g	Protein: 30.4 g
Fat: 20.3 g	Fiber: 2.3 g	Net Carbs: 6 g

FIRST PLACE CHILI

YIELD: 8 CUPS (1920 G)

SERVES 8 (1 CUP, OR
    240 G, EACH)

PREP TIME: 5M

COOK TIME: 24M

TOTAL TIME: 29M

1 pound (454 g) ground
    beef

3 ounces (84 g) chopped
    onion

3 ounces (84 g) chopped
    green bell pepper

3 tablespoons (21 g)
    ground cumin

1½ tablespoons (12 g)
    chili powder

2 teaspoons salt

1½ teaspoons garlic
    powder

¼ teaspoon ground
    coriander

¼ teaspoon cayenne
    pepper

Pinch of black pepper

½ cup (120 ml) water

1 can (28 ounces, or 784 g)
    crushed tomatoes

Everyone loves a good bowl of chili in the fall. Before we started eating low carb, I made chili all the time. I never measured anything, in true Southern Grandma fashion, but it always tasted so good. I adapted my old "recipe" when we adopted keto and won a (non-keto) chili cookoff, which is where the name First Place Chili was born!

Turn the pot to SAUTÉ mode. Once hot, add the beef and cook until it is mostly cooked through, 3 to 4 minutes. Use a wooden spoon to break up the beef into small pieces. Press CANCEL.

Add the onion, bell pepper, and spices and stir to combine. Add the water to the pot and stir to combine.

Add the tomatoes to the top of the beef mixture but do NOT stir.

Close the lid and seal the vent. Cook on HIGH pressure for 20 minutes. Quick release the steam.

Open the lid and stir the chili until thoroughly combined.

Complete the Meal: Maple Bacon Corn Bread (page 165)

MACRONUTRIENTS:

Calories: 195	Carbs: 10.5 g	Protein: 11.9 g
Fat: 11.6 g	Fiber: 3.3 g	Net Carbs: 7.2 g

FRENCH ONION SOUP

YIELD: 5½ CUPS
(1320 ML)

SERVES 10 (ABOUT
½ CUP, OR 120 ML,
EACH)

PREP TIME: 10M

COOK TIME: 35M

TOTAL TIME: 45M

1 ounce (28 g) butter

1 pound (454 g) chopped
onions (see Note)

6 cups (1440 ml) beef
broth

2 tablespoons (30 ml)
Worcestershire sauce

1 teaspoon dried thyme

1 teaspoon salt

Pinch of black pepper

Gruyère cheese, shredded
or sliced (optional)

French onion soup is a hearty beef broth loaded with caramelized onions that makes for a rich and satisfying meal. However, onions are high in carbs and can quickly eat up all of your macros for the day. This recipe is a toned-down version of the high-carb favorite. Serve it in small ramekins and top with Gruyère cheese for the full restaurant experience!

Turn the pot to SAUTÉ mode and add the butter. Once melted, add the onions and sauté until soft and translucent, 5 minutes. Alternatively, you may sauté the onions in a cast-iron skillet to fully caramelize them.

Press CANCEL. Add the broth, Worcestershire, thyme, salt, and pepper and stir to combine.

Close the lid and seal the vent. Cook on HIGH pressure for 30 minutes. Quick release the steam.

If desired, top each serving of soup with cheese and broil until brown and bubbly. This is not calculated in the macros.

Note: To ensure the correct macros for this recipe, weigh your onions *after* you've peeled and trimmed them. Start with about 18 ounces (504 g) of onions to account for the peels and trimmings.

MACRONUTRIENTS:

Calories: 121	Carbs: 5.5 g	Protein: 2.3 g
Fat: 1.2 g	Fiber: 0.8 g	Net Carbs: 4.7 g

TACO SOUP

YIELD: 7½ CUPS
(1800 ML)

SERVES 5 (1½ CUPS, OR
360 ML, EACH)

PREP TIME: 10M

COOK TIME: 34M

TOTAL TIME: 44M

1 pound (454 g) ground
beef

3½ ounces (100 g) diced
onion

2 cloves garlic, minced

1 tablespoon (7 g) ground
cumin

1 tablespoon (8 g) chili
powder

2 teaspoons dried
oregano

2 teaspoons salt

2 cups (480 ml) chicken
broth

1 can (14.5 ounces, or
406 g) diced tomatoes
with green chiles

3½ ounces (100 g) diced
green bell pepper

1 jalapeño, seeded
and diced

Switch things up on your next taco Tuesday and serve this soup instead. Top off your bowl with a few slices of avocado, a dollop of sour cream, some crumbled cotija cheese, and a sprinkle of fresh cilantro, and you'll have all the best parts of a taco in soup form.

Turn the pot to SAUTÉ mode. Once hot, add the ground beef and cook until most of the pink is gone, 3 to 4 minutes. Use a wooden spoon to break up the beef into small pieces as it cooks.

Add the onion and garlic and sauté until the beef is no longer pink, 3 to 4 minutes. Press CANCEL.

Add the cumin, chili powder, oregano, and salt and stir to coat. Add the broth, tomatoes (with juice), bell pepper, and jalapeño.

Close the lid and seal the vent. Cook on HIGH pressure for 30 minutes. Quick release the steam.

MACRONUTRIENTS:

Calories: 208	Carbs: 7.8 g	Protein: 19.4 g
Fat: 11.8 g	Fiber: 2.1 g	Net Carbs: 5.7 g

GEORGIA BRUNSWICK STEW

YIELD: 16 CUPS (3840 G)

SERVES 16 (1 CUP, OR
    240 G, EACH)

PREP TIME: 5M

COOK TIME: 30M

TOTAL TIME: 35M

This recipe is a nod to my home state. If you've ever been to a BBQ joint in Georgia, then you may have seen Brunswick stew on the menu. Think of it as a BBQ chili. It's hearty, sweet, and smoky and typically enjoyed as a side dish. I made the classic Brunswick stew keto friendly by omitting the starchy vegetables, roux, and sugar. You'll want a big batch of corn bread ready for this one!

1 cup (240 ml) chicken broth

1 pound (454 g) boneless, skinless chicken breasts (fresh or frozen)

1 pound (454 g) boneless pork chops (fresh or frozen)

1 teaspoon salt

½ teaspoon black pepper

12 ounces (340 g) frozen okra

5 ounces (140 g) chopped yellow onion (about 1 small onion)

1½ cups (360 ml) sugar-free BBQ sauce

1 can (28 ounces, or 784 g) crushed tomatoes

Pour the broth into the pot. Place the chicken breasts and pork chops inside.

Sprinkle the salt and pepper on top of the meat. Add the okra and onion.

Pour the BBQ sauce on top. Pour the crushed tomatoes on top of the sauce but do not stir the mixture.

Close the lid and seal the vent. Cook on HIGH pressure for 30 minutes. Quick release the steam.

Remove the lid. Use a slotted spoon to remove the pork chops and chicken breasts from the stew to a plate. Shred the meat with two forks and transfer back to the stew. Stir to combine.

Complete the Meal: Maple Bacon Corn Bread (page 165)
Coffee-Rubbed Pulled Pork (page 126)

MACRONUTRIENTS:

Calories: 121	Carbs: 7.2 g	Protein: 12.7 g
Fat: 4.1 g	Fiber: 1.5 g	Net Carbs: 5.7 g

RED WINE BEEF STEW

SERVES 10

PREP TIME: 10M

COOK TIME: 1H 15M

TOTAL TIME: 1H 25M

3½ pounds (1590 g) beef stew meat

1 pound (454 g) radishes, trimmed and cut in half

8 ounces (227 g) baby carrots

8 ounces (227 g) sliced baby bella mushrooms

5 ounces (140 g) chopped onion (about 1 small onion)

1 cup (150 g) frozen green peas

2 teaspoons salt

1½ teaspoons ground sage

1 teaspoon dried thyme

½ teaspoon dried oregano

½ teaspoon black pepper

1½ teaspoons garlic powder

2 bay leaves

3 cups (720 ml) beef broth

½ cup + 2 tablespoons (150 ml) dry red wine (such as Cabernet Sauvignon)

We're maxing out the Instant Pot with this beef stew, friends! Its deep flavors and aromatic spices will keep your tummy warm and full all winter long. Radishes replace potatoes in this dish; they are a magical vegetable for the ketogenic diet. When Old Man Winter makes his way to town this year, you'll be ready with this keto-friendly beef stew. Be sure to save room for a slice of Salted Caramel Pumpkin Cheesecake (page 188) for dessert.

Add the beef, radishes, carrots, mushrooms, onion, and peas to the pot.

Sprinkle the spices on top of the meat and vegetables. Place the bay leaves in the pot.

Pour in the broth and wine. Give it a good stir to make sure the spices are distributed throughout.

Close the lid and seal the vent. Cook on HIGH pressure for 50 minutes.

When the timer goes off, let the steam naturally release for 25 minutes before manually releasing.

Note: If you don't have dry red wine, you can use more beef broth instead. The red wine adds an amazing depth to the flavors, though, so I encourage you to try it.

MACRONUTRIENTS:

| Calories: 240 | Carbs: 9.2 g | Protein: 31.4 g |
| Fat: 7.3 g | Fiber: 2.4 g | Net Carbs: 6.8 g |

CHAPTER 6

Covered Dishes

Casseroles are comfort food at its finest. One-pot meals mean less cleanup, and who doesn't love that? Plus they are an easy way to sneak in fat and veggies to hit those macros. When my husband and I first got married, he refused to eat any kind of casserole. Now, my Spinach Artichoke Chicken Casserole (page 88) is one of his favorite meals! Using your Instant Pot to make casseroles is not as hard as it may seem. Two simple steps, and you're on your way to a delicious, healthy, and satisfying meal. Your Instant Pot will give your oven a break and let you spend extra time with the ones you love!

CHEESY CHICKEN AND CAULIFLOWER RICE

SERVES 5

PREP TIME: 5M

COOK TIME: 5M

TOTAL TIME: 10M

¼ cup (60 ml) water

15 ounces (3 cups, or 420 g) Shredded Chicken (page 114)

1 pound (454 g) riced cauliflower (fresh or frozen)

8 ounces (227 g) processed yellow melting cheese (such as Velveeta), cubed

2 ounces (56 g) cream cheese, cubed

2 tablespoons (28 g) butter

2 teaspoons Dijon mustard

1 teaspoon garlic powder

1 teaspoon salt

Pinch of black pepper

¼ cup (60 ml) heavy cream

Cauliflower is one of the most versatile vegetables on the planet. It can be used to make low-carb versions of pizza, potato salad, or mac and cheese. My favorite, riced cauliflower, is one of those items that I always have in bulk in my freezer. I toss it into all kinds of dishes to add nutrients and bulk up the volume. This Cheesy Chicken and Cauliflower Rice is the classic covered dish that we all grew up with and loved—only keto friendly.

Add the water to the pot. Place the shredded chicken inside. Pour the cauliflower rice on top of the chicken.

Add the yellow cheese, cream cheese, butter, mustard, garlic powder, salt, and pepper. Pour the cream on top of everything but do not stir.

Close the lid and seal the vent. Cook on LOW pressure for 5 minutes. Quick release the steam.

Remove the lid and stir the pot to incorporate all of the cheese into the mixture.

Note: If the processed cheese bothers you, substitute it with the same amount of shredded Cheddar cheese.

Complete the Meal: Southern-Style Green Beans (page 167)

MACRONUTRIENTS:

| Calories: 304 | Carbs: 9.9 g | Protein: 30.8 g |
| Fat: 15.4 g | Fiber: 2.2 g | Net Carbs: 7.7 g |

CHICKEN RO-TEL

SERVES 4

PREP TIME: 10M

COOK TIME: 20M

TOTAL TIME: 30M

3 tablespoons (42 g)
butter

5 ounces (140 g) diced
green bell pepper

4 ounces (112 g) sliced
mushrooms

1 pound (454 g)
cauliflower florets

8 ounces (227 g)
processed yellow
melting cheese (such as
Velveeta), cubed

1 cup (140 g) cooked
chicken

1 cup (150 g) green peas

1 can (10 ounces, or 280 g)
diced tomatoes with
green chiles, undrained

Pinch of salt

½ cup (120 ml) water

ACCESSORIES NEEDED:

7" (18 cm) baking dish

Trivet

Did you have a dish growing up that your mom always made special for you? For me, that was Chicken Ro-Tel. You may know it as "chicken spaghetti." Either way, it was not low carb. I replaced the spaghetti with cauliflower florets and omitted the onions to save carbs. This dish is a little higher in net carbs than others, but it's worth budgeting your carbs for the day to enjoy this for supper!

Turn the pot to SAUTÉ mode and add the butter. Once hot, add the pepper and mushrooms and sauté until soft and tender, 3 to 4 minutes. Press CANCEL.

Transfer the mixture to a large bowl. Add the cauliflower, cheese, chicken, peas, tomatoes, and salt and toss to combine. Pour the mixture into the baking dish and cover with aluminum foil.

Rinse the pot clean and add the water. Place the baking dish on the trivet and carefully lower it into the pot.

Close the lid and seal the vent. Cook on HIGH pressure for 15 minutes. Quick release the steam and remove.

MACRONUTRIENTS:

| Calories: 320 | Carbs: 18.2 g | Protein: 27 g |
| Fat: 15.5 g | Fiber: 4.1 g | Net Carbs: 12.1 g |

DECONSTRUCTED EGG ROLLS WITH PEANUT SAUCE

SERVES 4

PREP TIME: 10M

COOK TIME: 15M

TOTAL TIME: 25M

FOR "EGG ROLLS":

2 tablespoons (30 ml) sesame oil

1 pound (454 g) ground pork

¼ cup (60 ml) soy sauce (or coconut aminos)

¼ cup (60 ml) water

2 scallions, sliced, white and green parts kept separated

2 cloves garlic, minced

1½ teaspoons ground ginger

1 teaspoon salt

2 cups (4½ ounces, or 126 g) coleslaw mix

1 package (12 ounces, or 340 g) frozen cauliflower rice, prepared according to package directions

Chinese takeout has always been a guilty pleasure. The little white boxes, chopsticks, and fortune cookies add charisma to a simple meal. Adopting a ketogenic lifestyle meant I had to break up with our local Chinese food spot, but I replaced it with keto-friendly homemade options. This recipe is everything you love about a traditional egg roll, all the way down to the peanut butter on the wonton wrap.

To make the "egg rolls": Turn the pot to SAUTÉ mode and add the sesame oil. Once hot, add the pork.

Cook the pork, breaking it up into small pieces as it cooks. When the pork is just slightly pink, 3 to 4 minutes, press CANCEL.

Add the soy sauce, water, white parts of the scallions, garlic, ginger, and salt. Stir to combine. Add the coleslaw mix and stir once more.

Close the lid and seal the vent. Cook on LOW pressure for 5 minutes. Quick release the steam.

(ingredients and recipe continued on next page)

FOR PEANUT SAUCE:

- ¼ cup (65 g) peanut butter (no sugar or oil added)
- 2 tablespoons (30 ml) water
- 1½ tablespoons (23 ml) soy sauce
- 1½ teaspoons sriracha
- 1½ teaspoons sugar-free maple syrup
- 1 teaspoon lime juice

While the food is cooking, prepare the sauce: Place the peanut butter, water, soy sauce, sriracha, syrup, and lime juice in a food processor or blender and pulse until completely smooth.

Serve the egg rolls with the cauliflower rice and peanut sauce. Garnish with the reserved scallion greens.

Note: The peanut sauce is not very spicy, but you can start with ½ teaspoon sriracha and work your way up to 1½ teaspoons, if needed. Do not completely omit the sriracha.

MACRONUTRIENTS FOR THE "EGG ROLLS":

Calories: 414	Carbs: 7.8 g	Protein: 22.7 g
Fat: 30.8 g	Fiber: 2.9 g	Net Carbs: 4.9 g

MACRONUTRIENTS FOR THE PEANUT SAUCE:

Calories: 105	Carbs: 5.5 g	Protein: 4.3 g
Fat: 8 g	Fiber: 2.4 g	Net Carbs: 3.1 g

Total Net Carbs: 8 g

KENTUCKY HOT BROWN CASSEROLE

SERVES 4

PREP TIME: 5M

COOK TIME: 15M

TOTAL TIME: 25M

2 cups (280 g) cooked chicken or turkey

½ pound (227 g) bacon, cooked and chopped

4 ounces (112 g) diced tomatoes

2 tablespoons (28 g) butter

½ cup (120 ml) heavy cream

2 ounces (56 g) cream cheese, softened

½ cup (57 g) shredded extra-sharp white Cheddar cheese

½ cup (120 ml) water

ACCESSORIES NEEDED:

7" (18 cm) baking dish

Trivet

A Kentucky Hot Brown is a famous open-face sandwich that hails from the Brown Hotel in Louisville, Kentucky. Sourdough bread is topped with baked turkey, ham, bacon, tomato, and a béchamel gravy. It's a favorite around this part of the country but very unfriendly for a ketogenic diet. This casserole is my keto version of it. I added the extra-sharp white Cheddar for a little zing. This one will have you singing "My Old Kentucky Home" before supper is over!

Place the chicken, bacon, and tomatoes in the baking dish and set aside.

Turn the pot to SAUTÉ mode and add the butter. Once melted, add the cream. Whisk continuously as it warms up.

When the butter and cream mixture begins to bubble and foam up, add the cream cheese and whisk until it is completely melted and there are no clumps. Add the Cheddar cheese and whisk until melted and smooth. Press CANCEL.

Pour the cheese sauce on top of the chicken mixture. Carefully fold the mixture until evenly combined.

Rinse the pot clean and add the water. Place the baking dish on the trivet and carefully lower the trivet into the pot.

Close the lid and seal the vent. Cook on HIGH pressure for 10 minutes. Quick release the steam.

Carefully remove the trivet from the pot. Let the casserole rest for 5 minutes before serving.

MACRONUTRIENTS:

Calories: 642	Carbs: 2.1 g	Protein: 52.6 g
Fat: 45.6 g	Fiber: 0.4 g	Net Carbs: 1.7 g

ENCHILADA CASSEROLE

SERVES 4

PREP TIME: 10M

COOK TIME: 20M

TOTAL TIME: 35M

I've never met a taco, enchilada, or quesadilla I didn't like, and this casserole recipe marries two foods that we all love: enchiladas and casseroles. Top with a dollop of sour cream, lettuce, and tomato, and serve it up with Mexican Cauliflower Rice (page 20) for a Mexican feast.

1 pound (454 g) ground beef

1½ teaspoons chili powder

1 teaspoon ground cumin

1 teaspoon garlic powder

1 teaspoon salt

½ teaspoon onion powder

¼ teaspoon smoked paprika

⅓ cup (80 ml) red enchilada sauce

¼ cup (60 g) sour cream

Cooking spray

4 low-carb tortillas

1½ cups (175 g) shredded Mexican cheese blend

½ cup (120 ml) water

ACCESSORIES NEEDED:

7" (18 cm) baking dish

Trivet

Turn the pot to SAUTÉ mode. Once hot, cook the beef until mostly cooked through, 3 to 4 minutes, breaking up the pieces of meat with a wooden spoon.

Add the spices and cook until the meat is cooked through, 1 to 2 minutes. Transfer the meat to a bowl. Press CANCEL.

In a small bowl, combine the enchilada sauce and sour cream.

Grease the bottom of the baking dish with cooking spray. Place one tortilla inside. If the tortilla is slightly larger than the dish, flatten the edges along the sides of the dish.

Add one-third of the taco meat on top of the tortilla. Spread one-third of the enchilada sauce mixture on top of the meat. Add one-fourth of the cheese on top.

Repeat the layers two more times. Top the last tortilla with the remaining one-fourth cheese.

Cover the dish tightly with aluminum foil. Add the water to the pot. Set the baking dish on top of the trivet and carefully lower it into the pot.

Close the lid and seal the vent. Cook on HIGH pressure for 10 minutes. Quick release the steam.

Remove the dish from the pot. Let sit for 5 minutes before cutting into the pie.

Note: If you are gluten free, you can replace the low-carb tortillas with thinly sliced zucchini. Make sure the zucchini has been dried properly so that the dish does not become watery. You will need to recalculate the macros.

MACRONUTRIENTS:

Calories: 558
Fat: 36.9 g

Carbs: 23 g
Fiber: 13.8 g

Protein: 38.7 g
Net Carbs: 10.8 g

POPPY SEED CHICKEN

SERVES 4

PREP TIME: 5M

COOK TIME: 15M

TOTAL TIME: 20M

3 cups (420 g) cooked
chicken or Roast
Chicken (page 115)

1 cup (240 ml) Homemade
Cream of Chicken Soup
(page 67)

½ cup (120 g) sour cream

2 teaspoons poppy seeds

½ teaspoon garlic powder

½ teaspoon salt

½ cup (120 ml) water

¾ cup (112 ounces, or
42 g) crushed pork
rinds

1 tablespoon (14 g) butter,
melted

ACCESSORIES NEEDED:

7" (18 cm) baking dish

Trivet

This casserole recipe is a nod to an old Southern classic that my mom used to fix us growing up. Her version used canned cream of chicken soup and buttery snack crackers, but I've transformed it into a keto-friendly covered dish. Serve it to house guests, carry it to a sick friend, or take it to the church potluck for a low-carb comfort meal!

Heat the broiler.

In a medium bowl, combine the chicken, soup, sour cream, poppy seeds, garlic powder, and salt.

Transfer to the baking dish and cover tightly with aluminum foil.

Add the water to the pot. Place the baking dish on the trivet and carefully lower it into the pot.

Close the lid and seal the vent. Cook on HIGH pressure for 10 minutes. Quick release the steam.

Meanwhile, in a small bowl, mix the pork rinds and melted butter.

Remove the foil and spread the pork rinds on top of the casserole. Place under the broiler until crisp, about 5 minutes.

Note: Store-bought rotisserie chicken can make this a super-fast weeknight meal. You may swap the homemade cream of chicken soup for the canned version. If you do so, recalculate the macros for the most accurate numbers.

Complete the Meal: Broccoli with Garlic-Herb Cheese Sauce (page 158) Southern-Style Green Beans (page 167)

MACRONUTRIENTS:

| Calories: 408 | Carbs: 2.5 g | Protein: 34.9 g |
| Fat: 28.3 g | Fiber: 0.5 g | Net Carbs: 2 g |

SPINACH ARTICHOKE CHICKEN CASSEROLE

SERVES 6

PREP TIME: 5M

COOK TIME: 5M

TOTAL TIME: 10M

½ cup (120 ml) chicken broth

1 pound (454 g) cooked chicken or Roast Chicken (page 115), shredded

1 pound (454 g) frozen broccoli florets

16 ounces (454 g) store-bought spinach artichoke dip

¾ cup (75 g) grated Parmesan cheese

I love a made-from-scratch recipe, but some nights I need a meal that I can throw together in 5 minutes and call it a day. That's when the recipe for this casserole comes in to play. A store-bought spinach artichoke dip becomes a melty, warm, and satisfying casserole in 5 minutes! Sneak in some broccoli and you have a well-balanced keto casserole.

Pour the broth into the pot.

Add the chicken to the pot. Put the broccoli on top but do not stir.

Add the spinach artichoke dip on top. To prevent the bottom from scorching, do not stir the mixture.

Close the lid and seal the vent. Cook on LOW pressure for 5 minutes. Quick release the steam.

Add the cheese and give it a gentle stir to incorporate all of the melted dip and broccoli. If your broccoli breaks into really small pieces, that's okay. (Your kids will never know it's in there!)

Optional: Top with 1 cup (115 g) shredded mozzarella cheese and place under the broiler for 5 minutes. (This step is not included in the macros.)

MACRONUTRIENTS:

| Calories: 387 | Carbs: 10.4 g | Protein: 28.3 g |
| Fat: 26.9 g | Fiber: 2 g | Net Carbs: 8.4 g |

CRUSTLESS CHICKEN POT PIE

SERVES 4

PREP TIME: 5M

COOK TIME: 15M

TOTAL TIME: 20M

Homemade chicken pot pie is surely one of the most comforting and classic casseroles of all time. Most people find that once they become fat adapted, they genuinely do not miss eating refined carbs. It's possible to enjoy all of your favorite foods without the carb coma that used to follow suit. This pot pie is a savory casserole full of healthy fat and protein and low in carbs.

2 cups (280 g) cooked chicken or Roast Chicken (page 115)

1 bag (12½ ounces, or 350 g) frozen green beans

5 ounces (140 g) chopped carrots

2 tablespoons (28 g) butter

1 cup (240 ml) heavy cream

¾ cup (180 ml) chicken broth

¾ teaspoon xanthan gum

½ teaspoon garlic powder

½ teaspoon dried thyme

½ teaspoon ground sage

½ cup (120 ml) water

ACCESSORIES NEEDED:

7" (18 cm) baking dish

Trivet

In a medium bowl, combine the chicken, green beans, and carrots.

Turn the pot to SAUTÉ mode and add the butter. When melted, add the cream. Whisk occasionally as the mixture heats up.

When the cream begins to bubble around the edges, add the broth, xanthan gum, garlic powder, thyme, and sage. Whisk continuously until a thin sauce has formed. This should take no more than 5 minutes.

When the sauce has thickened, pour it into the bowl with the chicken mixture. Press CANCEL. Stir thoroughly to coat the chicken and vegetables with the sauce.

Transfer the mixture to the baking dish. Rinse out the pot and add the water.

Place the baking dish on the trivet and carefully lower the trivet into the pot. Close the lid and seal the vent. Cook on HIGH pressure for 10 minutes. Quick release the steam.

Complete the Meal: Maple Bacon Corn Bread (page 165)
Double Chocolate Chip Brownies (page 185)

MACRONUTRIENTS:

| Calories: 329 | Carbs: 12.6 g | Protein: 27.1 g |
| Fat: 18.7 g | Fiber: 5.4 g | Net Carbs: 7.2 g |

CHAPTER 7

Beef

Of all the animal proteins, beef is my absolute favorite. I love a juicy steak just as much as a meatloaf. Beef has so much flavor, especially when you purchase grass-fed meat, and it is also an excellent food choice on a ketogenic diet. Beef is full of healthy fat and protein, which makes it ideal for meeting those macros. Use your Instant Pot as the perfect vessel for juicy, flavorful, and tender cuts of beef every time.

SHREDDED BEEF

SERVES 6

PREP TIME: 2M

COOK TIME: 1H 10M

TOTAL TIME: 1H 12M

2 pounds (908 g) top
    round roast

½ cup (120 ml) beef broth

2 teaspoons (12 g) salt

1 teaspoon black pepper

3 whole cloves garlic

1 bay leaf

Shredded beef is a great food to keep stocked in your freezer. Make a batch to keep on hand for sandwiches, soups, enchiladas, tacos, or whatever else your keto heart desires. Using a top round roast for this recipe will allow you to shred the beef with two forks or slice it into very thin pieces. If you have a batch of Bone Broth (page 93) on hand, you can sub it for the beef broth and pack in an extra dose of nutrients!

Add the roast, broth, salt, pepper, garlic, and bay leaf to the pot.

Close the lid and seal the vent. Cook on HIGH pressure for 15 minutes. Let the steam naturally release for 15 minutes before manually releasing.

Remove the beef from the pot and slice or shred it. Store it in an airtight container in the fridge or freezer.

MACRONUTRIENTS:

Calories: 178	Carbs: 0.8 g	Protein: 31.7 g
Fat: 4.3 g	Fiber: 0.1 g	Net Carbs: 0.7 g

BONE BROTH

YIELD: VARIES

PREP TIME: 50M

COOK TIME: 2H

TOTAL TIME: 2H 50M

4 pounds (1816 g) beef marrow bones

1 tablespoon (18 g) salt

1 teaspoon black pepper

5 cloves garlic

4 bay leaves

2 tablespoons (30 ml) apple cider vinegar

Bone broth has long been known for its healing properties, but it tends to be quite pricey at the grocery store. Don't fret; it is extremely affordable to make in your Instant Pot. A stovetop batch of bone broth can take up to 48 hours to make, but your Instant Pot gets the job done in just 2 hours! Be sure to buy high-quality grass-fed bones to yield the highest quality broth. You may also customize your broth with your favorite herbs and spices.

Heat the oven to 425°F (220°C, or gas mark 7). Lay the bones on a baking sheet and roast for 45 minutes.

Remove the bones from the oven and place them in the Instant Pot. Add the salt, pepper, garlic, and bay leaves.

Fill the pot with water to the fill line. Add the apple cider vinegar.

Close the lid and seal the vent. Cook on HIGH pressure for 2 hours. Quick release the steam.

Use a fine-mesh sieve to strain the broth into jars. Store unused broth in the freezer.

Note: Upon cooling, your broth will turn to jelly. The more jelly you see, the more collagen was extracted from the bones during cooking. The gel will turn to liquid once it is reheated.

MACRONUTRIENTS:

Macros are not included for this recipe. The amount of fat and protein extracted from the bones will vary, as will the final amount of broth produced. You may calculate the macros for your batch of bone broth using a fitness tracker app.

BABY BACK RIBS WITH BBQ GLAZE

SERVES 4

PREP TIME: 10M

COOK TIME: 35M

TOTAL TIME: 45M

½ cup (120 ml) water

1 rack beef back ribs (about 3 pounds, or 1362 g), prepared with rub of choice

¼ cup (60 g) sugar-free ketchup

3 tablespoons (45 ml) sugar-free maple syrup

2 teaspoons apple cider vinegar

35 drops liquid smoke

¼ teaspoon Worcestershire sauce

¼ teaspoon garlic powder

¼ teaspoon smoked paprika

Dash of cayenne pepper (or more, for spicier sauce)

ACCESSORY NEEDED:

Trivet

Put away the smokers, y'all. These baby back ribs are so easy to make and fall-off-the-bone tender that you'll never want to make them any other way. No more fussin' over hot smoke, flipping, and basting. Your Instant Pot will cook your ribs perfectly in about half an hour. Grab a glass of iced tea and cheers to that!

Pour the water in the pot and place the trivet inside.

Arrange the ribs on top of the trivet with the underside of the ribs facing the lining of the pot. The meat should be facing the inside of the pot.

Close the lid and seal the vent. Cook on HIGH pressure for 25 minutes.

While the ribs are cooking, prepare the glaze by whisking together the ketchup, maple syrup, vinegar, liquid smoke, Worcestershire sauce, garlic powder, paprika, and cayenne in a medium bowl.

Heat the broiler.

Quick release the steam. Remove the ribs and place on a baking sheet.

Brush a thick layer of glaze on the ribs with a basting brush. Put under the broiler for 5 minutes.

Remove from the broiler and brush with glaze again. Put back under the broiler for 5 more minutes, or until the tops are sticky.

Note: Macros are approximations, as the edible portion of meat per rib will vary. To ensure accuracy, weigh the meat before consumption and use a fitness app to calculate the nutritional information.

MACRONUTRIENTS FOR SAUCE:

Calories: 37	Carbs: 11.8 g	Protein: 0.1 g
Fat: 0.1 g	Fiber: 8.3 g	Net Carbs: 3.5 g

MACRONUTRIENTS FOR RIBS:

Calories: 630	Carbs: 0 g	Protein: 44.3 g
Fat: 51.3 g	Fiber: 0 g	Net Carbs: 0 g

Total Net Carbs: 3.5 g

BACON AND CHEDDAR–STUFFED BURGERS

SERVES 4

PREP TIME: 10M

COOK TIME: 9M

TOTAL TIME: 19M

1 pound (454 g) ground beef

6 ounces (168 g) shredded Cheddar cheese

5 slices bacon, coarsely chopped

2 teaspoons Worcestershire sauce

1 teaspoon salt

½ teaspoon liquid smoke

½ teaspoon black pepper

½ teaspoon garlic powder

1 cup (240 ml) water

ACCESSORY NEEDED:

Trivet

Bacon cheeseburgers are a quintessential American food, and it's just as easy to make burgers in the Instant Pot as it is to go to a drive-through. I like to serve our burgers in lettuce wraps with all the fixin's. The kids like to skip the lettuce and dip their burgers in a little sugar-free ketchup. You can make a whole batch of these and have burgers prepped for a busy week or for lunchboxes.

In a large bowl, add the beef, cheese, bacon, Worcestershire sauce, salt, liquid smoke, pepper, and garlic powder. Gently work everything into the meat. Do not overwork the meat, or it will become tough when it cooks.

Separate the meat into four equal portions. Use a food scale to measure evenly.

Shape each piece into a ball. Use your thumb to make a crater in the middle of the patty but make sure the round shape is retained.

Wrap each patty loosely in aluminum foil. Place them on top of the trivet in the pot. They will overlap.

Add the water to the bottom of the pot. Close the lid and seal the vent. Cook on HIGH pressure for 9 minutes. Quick release the steam.

Remove the foil packets from the pot and set them on a large plate. Carefully unwrap the burgers. There will be juices in the bottom of the foil.

Complete the Meal: Bacon Jelly (page 156)

MACRONUTRIENTS:

Calories: 454	Carbs: 2.4 g	Protein: 38.6 g
Fat: 33.5 g	Fiber: 0.1 g	Net Carbs: 2.3 g

TAKE-OUT STYLE BEEF AND BROCCOLI

SERVES 6

PREP TIME: 10M

COOK TIME: 12M

TOTAL TIME: 22M

½ cup (120 ml) soy sauce (or coconut aminos)

¼ cup (60 ml) beef broth

¼ cup (60 ml) water

2 scallions, thinly sliced, plus more for garnish if desired

1 tablespoon (15 ml) fish sauce

1 tablespoon (12 g) powdered erythritol

2 teaspoons garlic powder

1½ teaspoons ginger paste

1½ pounds (680 g) flank steak, sliced into very thin strips (less than ½", or 13 mm, thick)

2 pounds (908 g) broccoli florets

½ teaspoon xanthan gum

If Chinese takeout was your favorite way to cap off a long workweek before you went keto, then this recipe is for you! It has all the flavors of traditional takeout without the junk and carbs. Add a little flair to your fake-out takeout night by serving your meal in Chinese paper boxes with chopsticks.

In a small bowl, whisk together the soy sauce, broth, water, scallions, fish sauce, sweetener, garlic powder, and ginger paste.

Pour into the pot, and add the beef. Close the lid and seal the vent. Cook on HIGH pressure for 10 minutes. Quick release the steam.

Meanwhile, steam the broccoli florets by placing them in a microwave-safe bowl with 2 to 3 tablespoons (30 to 45 ml) of water. Cover with plastic wrap and microwave until the broccoli is crisp-tender, 3 to 4 minutes.

Remove the meat with a slotted spoon and place in a bowl. Cover with aluminum foil to keep warm.

Turn the pot to SAUTÉ mode. Let the sauce come to a low boil and add the xanthan gum. Whisk continuously until the sauce is slightly sticky or stretchy, about 2 minutes.

Add the broccoli to the beef. Pour the sauce over the meat and broccoli. If desired, garnish with additional scallion greens.

Note: If there are little pieces of meat left in the broth after cooking, you may run it through a fine-mesh sieve before making the sauce.

MACRONUTRIENTS:

Calories: 241	Carbs: 8.9 g	Protein: 28.9 g
Fat: 9 g	Fiber: 3.5 g	Net Carbs: 5.4 g

BEEF STROGANOFF MEATBALLS

SERVES 4 (6 MEATBALLS
EACH)

PREP TIME: 10M

COOK TIME: 14M

TOTAL TIME: 24M

1 pound (454 g) ground
    beef

1 egg

4 tablespoons (60 ml)
    heavy cream, divided

3 cloves garlic, minced

1 tablespoon (4 g)
    chopped fresh parsley,
    plus more for garnish

½ teaspoon salt

Pinch of black pepper

1 cup (240) beef broth

8 ounces (227 g) sliced
    baby bella mushrooms

¼ cup (60 g) sour cream

1 teaspoon xanthan gum

If you're a fan of the Swedish meatballs at IKEA, then you're going to adore this recipe! Whether you call it beef Stroganoff or Swedish meatballs, these meatballs are divine. A sour cream gravy on a bed of herby meatballs is all you need to wind down after a hectic day. Serve these alongside a batch of Homemade Egg Noodles (page 19), spaghetti squash, or zucchini noodles for a full meal the whole family will love.

In a large bowl, combine the beef, egg, 2 tablespoons (30 ml) of the heavy cream, garlic, parsley, salt, and pepper. Use a spoon to work everything evenly into the beef.

Use a cookie scoop to divide out 24 meatballs, about 1 ounce (28 g) each. Roll them between your hands to round them out.

Add the broth and mushrooms to the pot. Place the meatballs on top of the mushrooms.

Close the lid and seal the vent. Cook on HIGH pressure for 12 minutes. Quick release the steam. Press CANCEL.

Use a slotted spoon to transfer the meatballs from the pot to a bowl or platter.

Turn the pot to SAUTÉ mode. Whisk in the sour cream and the remaining 2 tablespoons (30 ml) heavy cream. Once the broth begins to lightly boil, whisk in the xanthan gum. Continue whisking until a thin gravy consistency is reached, about 2 minutes. Pour the gravy on top of the meatballs. Garnish with fresh parsley.

MACRONUTRIENTS:

Calories: 408	Carbs: 13.8 g	Protein: 28.8 g
Fat: 27.2 g	Fiber: 7.2 g	Net Carbs: 6.6 g

BEEF TENDERLOIN WITH RED WINE REDUCTION

SERVES 5

PREP TIME: 35M

COOK TIME: 10M

TOTAL TIME: 55M

2 pounds (908 g) beef tenderloin

Salt

Black pepper

2 tablespoons (30 ml) avocado oil

½ cup (120 ml) beef broth

½ cup (120 ml) dry red wine (such as Cabernet Sauvignon)

2 cloves garlic, minced

1 teaspoon Worcestershire sauce

1½ teaspoons dried rosemary

¼ teaspoon xanthan gum

Chopped fresh rosemary, for garnish (optional)

The Instant Pot isn't just for making chili and pot roast. *Au contraire!* Your Instant Pot can cook tender and high-quality cuts of meat without the need for babysitting the oven. It gives you extra time to enjoy a glass of champagne while you wait! Beef tenderloin is an expensive cut of meat—it's where filet mignon comes from—but when cooked properly, it's worth every penny. This recipe will yield a perfectly medium-rare steak fit for a king or Christmas dinner!

Thirty minutes prior to cooking, take the tenderloin out of the fridge and let it come to room temperature. Crust the outside of the tenderloin in salt and pepper.

Turn the pot to SAUTÉ mode and add the avocado oil. Once hot, add the tenderloin and sear on all sides, about 5 minutes. Press CANCEL.

Add the broth, wine, garlic, Worcestershire sauce, and rosemary to the pot around the beef.

Close the lid and seal the vent. Cook on HIGH pressure for 8 minutes. Quick release the steam.

Remove the tenderloin to a platter, tent with aluminum foil, and let it rest for 10 minutes. Press CANCEL.

Turn the pot to SAUTÉ mode. Once the broth has begun a low boil, add the xanthan gum and whisk until a thin sauce has formed, 2 to 3 minutes.

Slice the tenderloin against the grain into thin rounds. Top each slice with the red wine glaze. Garnish with rosemary, if desired.

Complete the Meal: Easy Lobster Tails (page 125)
Rosemary Mushrooms (page 163)
Horseradish Whipped Cauliflower (page 162)

MACRONUTRIENTS:

Calories: 575	Carbs: 2 g	Protein: 32.6 g
Fat: 44.1 g	Fiber: 0.9 g	Net Carbs: 1.1 g

CARNE ASADA BITES

SERVES 4

PREP TIME: 40M

COOK TIME: 5M

TOTAL TIME: 45M

2½ ounces (70 g) diced red onion

2 chipotle peppers in adobo plus sauce

Juice of 2 limes

2 tablespoons (2 g) chopped fresh cilantro

2 cloves garlic, minced

1½ teaspoons ground cumin

1 teaspoon salt

1 pound (454 g) skirt steak or flat iron steak, cut into 1" (2.5 cm) strips, then into bite-size pieces

¼ cup (60 ml) beef broth

Carne asada is Spanish for "roasted meat," but we're going to pretend it means pressure-cooked meat! These steak bites are a quick, no-fuss way to serve your favorite street-style taco. The Instant Pot makes the meat incredibly tender and flavorful. You can serve these in low-carb tortillas, in lettuce cups, or on a bed of Mexican Cauliflower Rice (page 20). I like to top them with pico de gallo, guacamole, and cheese.

In a small bowl, combine the onion, chipotles and sauce, lime juice, cilantro, garlic, cumin, and salt. Use a meat masher to mash up the mixture. You may also use a mortar and pestle or a food processor (but do not puree the marinade).

Transfer the marinade to a resealable plastic bag, along with the steak. Marinate in the refrigerator for 30 minutes.

Remove the steak from the refrigerator. Pour the contents of the bag into the Instant Pot. Add the broth.

Close the lid and seal the vent. Cook on HIGH pressure for 5 minutes. Quick release the steam and remove.

MACRONUTRIENTS:

| Calories: 240 | Carbs: 4.5 g | Protein: 22.8 g |
| Fat: 14.3 g | Fiber: 0.5 g | Net Carbs: 4 g |

FRENCH DIP ROAST BEEF

SERVES 6

PREP TIME: 5M

COOK TIME: 1H 10M

TOTAL TIME: 1H 15M

2 tablespoons (30 ml) avocado oil

2 to 2½ pounds (908 to 1135 g) chuck roast

2 cups (480 ml) beef broth

2 tablespoons (6 g) dried rosemary

3 cloves garlic, minced

1 teaspoon salt

½ teaspoon black pepper

¼ teaspoon dried thyme

½ onion, quartered

2 bay leaves

Despite its name, the French dip is actually an American-inspired dish. Traditionally served on a French roll, keto French dips can be served on your favorite low-carb or Fat Head rolls (see page 18). You can skip the "bread" altogether and just top them with sautéed mushrooms and melted Swiss cheese. Either way, be sure to dip them in the *jus* (literally "juice" in French).

Turn the pot to SAUTÉ mode. Once hot, add the avocado oil. Add the roast and sear it on each side. This should take about 5 minutes. Press CANCEL.

Add the broth to the pot.

Add the rosemary, garlic, salt, pepper, and thyme to the top of the roast. Add the onion and bay leaves.

Close the lid and seal the vent. Cook on HIGH pressure for 50 minutes. Let the steam naturally release for 15 minutes before manually releasing.

Remove the roast to a plate and shred with two forks. Strain the jus though a fine-mesh sieve. Serve the roast *au jus* for dipping.

Complete the Meal: Creamed Spinach (page 157)
Horseradish Whipped Cauliflower (page 162)

MACRONUTRIENTS:

Calories: 548	Carbs: 2.2 g	Protein: 55.4 g
Fat: 34.2 g	Fiber: 0.7 g	Net Carbs: 1.5 g

ITALIAN MEATLOAF

SERVES 6

PREP TIME: 10M

COOK TIME: 25M

TOTAL TIME: 35M

When I think about American food, meatloaf always comes to mind. There are so many ways to make it. This recipe combines a love for spaghetti and meatballs with a love for meatloaf. It's bursting with flavor, and it's a wonderful dish to satisfy cravings for carby Italian food.

1 pound (454 g) ground beef

1 cup (2 ounces, or 56 g) crushed pork rinds

1 egg

¼ cup (25 g) grated Parmesan cheese

¼ cup (60 ml) Italian dressing

2 teaspoons Italian seasoning

½ cup (120 ml) water

½ cup (120 g) sugar-free ketchup

1 tablespoon (4 g) chopped fresh herbs (such as parsley or basil)

1 clove garlic, minced

ACCESSORY NEEDED:

Trivet

In large bowl, combine the beef, pork rinds, egg, cheese, dressing, and Italian seasoning. Use a wooden spoon to incorporate everything into the meat, but do not overwork the meat or it will turn out tough.

Turn the meat mixture out onto a piece of aluminum foil. Use your hands to shape into a loaf. Wrap the foil up around the meat like a packet, but do not cover the top. Place the trivet in the pot and add the water. Place the meatloaf on top of the trivet.

Close the lid and seal the vent. Cook on HIGH pressure 20 minutes. Quick release the steam.

While the meat is cooking, whisk together the ketchup, herbs, and garlic in a small bowl. Heat the broiler.

Remove the meat and foil packet from the pot. Place on a baking sheet and spread the ketchup mixture on top.

Broil until the glaze becomes sticky, about 5 minutes. Slice into six equal pieces.

Optional: After glazing the meatloaf with the ketchup mixture, sprinkle shredded mozzarella cheese on top and broil until melted and bubbly. (This is not calculated in the macros.)

Complete the Meal: Creamed Spinach (page 157)

MACRONUTRIENTS:

Calories: 358	Carbs: 2.3 g	Protein: 29.2 g
Fat: 25.2 g	Fiber: 0 g	Net Carbs: 2.3 g

ITALIAN POT ROAST WITH GIARDINIERA GRAVY

SERVES 6

PREP TIME: 5M

COOK TIME: 60M

TOTAL TIME: 1H 15M

½ cup (120 ml) beef broth

½ cup (120 ml) liquid from giardiniera mix

2½ pounds (1135 g) chuck roast

1 teaspoon garlic powder

1 teaspoon dried parsley

1 teaspoon dried oregano

½ teaspoon salt

½ teaspoon black pepper

½ cup (65 g) giardiniera mix

½ cup (112 g) butter, cut into cubes

1 teaspoon xanthan gum

This pot roast is not your average Sunday supper. Processed, carb-laden spice packets are replaced by an Italian-style pickled vegetable mix called giardiniera. You can find jarred giardiniera mix in the same aisle as pickles and condiments at your grocery store. This roast will have you singing "That's Amore"!

Pour the beef broth and giardiniera liquid into the pot.

Lay the roast in the pot. If it's too large to lie flat, cut it into smaller sections.

In a small bowl, mix the spices and sprinkle on top of the roast. Put the giardiniera mix and butter pats on top.

Close the lid and seal the vent. Cook on HIGH pressure for 55 minutes. Quick release the steam. Press CANCEL.

Remove the roast to a plate. Shred with two forks. Cover with aluminum foil until ready to serve.

Turn the pot to SAUTÉ mode. Let the broth come to a low boil. Sprinkle in the xanthan gum and whisk continuously. Allow the sauce to cook until thickened to a gravy consistency, 3 to 4 minutes. Pour the gravy over the shredded roast, reserving some for serving.

Note: If desired, add 1 pound (454 g) baby carrots or radishes around the edges of the roast while cooking. You will need to recalculate the macros.

Complete the Meal: Horseradish Whipped Cauliflower (page 162)

MACRONUTRIENTS:

| Calories: 669 | Carbs: 3.6 g | Protein: 42 g |
| Fat: 52.7 g | Fiber: 2.4 g | Net Carbs: 1.2 g |

PHILLY CHEESESTEAK–STUFFED PEPPERS

SERVES 4

PREP TIME: 10M

COOK TIME: 8M

TOTAL TIME: 18M

1 tablespoon (14 g) butter

1 pound (454 g) shaved beef

4 ounces (112 g) mushrooms, coarsely chopped

2½ ounces (70 g) sliced onion

1 tablespoon (15 ml) Worcestershire sauce

1 teaspoon seasoned salt

¼ teaspoon salt

¼ teaspoon black pepper

4 large bell peppers (any color)

½ cup (120 ml) water

4 slices provolone cheese

ACCESSORY NEEDED:

Trivet

I've never been to Philadelphia or eaten an authentic cheesesteak, but I do know all the words to "Fresh Prince of Bel-Air," so that counts for something, right? You won't even miss the bread when the shaved beef and mushrooms are stuffed into tender peppers. Stuffed peppers are a big thing in the Midwest, so it felt appropriate to incorporate them into the book—and they cook so much faster in the Instant Pot.

Heat the broiler.

Turn the pot to SAUTÉ mode and add the butter. Once melted, add the beef, mushrooms, and onion. Sauté until softened, 2 to 3 minutes. Add the Worcestershire sauce, seasoned salt, salt, and black pepper. Stir to evenly combine. Press CANCEL.

Slice the tops off the bell peppers and remove the cores and seeds. Fill each pepper with 4¼ ounces (120 g) of the meat mixture. Rinse out the pot.

Place the pot back into the base. Add the water and the trivet. Place the peppers on top of the trivet.

Close the lid and seal the vent. Cook on HIGH pressure for 5 minutes. Quick release the steam.

Carefully remove the trivet from the pot. Transfer the peppers to a baking sheet. Place one slice of provolone cheese on top of each pepper and broil for about 1 minute to melt the cheese.

MACRONUTRIENTS:

| Calories: 294 | Carbs: 5.2 g | Protein: 25.6 g |
| Fat: 18.3 g | Fiber: 0.6 g | Net Carbs: 4.6 g |

UN-SLOPPY JOES

SERVES 6

PREP TIME: 5M

COOK TIME: 15M

TOTAL TIME: 20M

1 pound (454 g) ground
beef

½ cup (120 g) sugar-free
ketchup

¼ cup (64 g) brown sugar
substitute

1 tablespoon (11 g) yellow
mustard

1 tablespoon (15 g) sugar-
free BBQ sauce

2 teaspoons apple cider
vinegar

¼ teaspoon salt

They're messy and stain your fingers orange, but I love the way a Sloppy Joe can transport me back to simpler times. These days, I avoid the wet wipes by skipping the bun and opting for a fork. Serve alongside a salad and Faux Mac and Cheese (page 161) for a keto-friendly guilty pleasure.

Turn the pot to SAUTÉ mode. Add the beef and brown it, breaking it up with a wooden spoon as it cooks. Press CANCEL once the meat is cooked most of the way through, 3 to 4 minutes. Do not drain the grease. (If you do want to drain the grease, add ¼ cup, or 60 ml, water to the mixture before cooking.)

Add the ketchup, brown sugar substitute, mustard, BBQ sauce, vinegar, and salt. Stir to combine.

Close the lid and seal the vent. Cook on HIGH pressure for 10 minutes. Quick release the steam.

MACRONUTRIENTS:

Calories: 176	Carbs: 1.7 g	Protein: 14.5 g
Fat: 11.4 g	Fiber: 0.1 g	Net Carbs: 1.6 g

SALISBURY STEAK

SERVES 4

PREP TIME: 10M

COOK TIME: 25M

TOTAL TIME: 35M

1 pound (454 g) ground
   beef

4 teaspoons (20 ml)
   Worcestershire sauce

1 tablespoon (15 g) sugar-
   free ketchup

2 teaspoons dried parsley

1 teaspoon salt

1 teaspoon black pepper

½ teaspoon yellow
   mustard

8 ounces (227 g) sliced
   baby bella mushrooms

3 ounces (84 g) thinly
   sliced onion

2 cups (480 ml) beef broth

¼ cup (60 ml) water

3 tablespoons (21 g)
   arrowroot powder

Chopped fresh parsley,
   for garnish

Salisbury steak always makes me think of a 1950s TV dinner. I consider it one of those retro meals that are always served at hole-in-the-wall diners. Well, not anymore! This ketofied Salisbury steak is low in carbs but high in nostalgia. Serve this steak with Horseradish Whipped Cauliflower (page 162) for a comforting home-style meal.

In a large bowl, combine the beef, Worcestershire sauce, ketchup, parsley, salt, pepper, and mustard. Make sure everything is evenly combined.

Shape the beef into four large oval patties, about ¾" (1.8 cm) thick. Place the patties into the pot. Place the mushrooms and onion on top of the patties. Add the broth to the pot.

Close the lid and seal the vent. Cook on HIGH pressure for 15 minutes. Quick release the steam. Press CANCEL.

Remove the patties, mushrooms, and onions with a slotted spoon or spatula.

Make a slurry by whisking together the water and arrowroot in a small measuring cup.

Turn the pot to SAUTÉ mode. When the broth comes to a low boil, whisk in the slurry. Continue whisking until a gravy has formed, 5 to 10 minutes. Pour the gravy over the patties. Garnish with parsley before serving.

MACRONUTRIENTS:

| Calories: 286 | Carbs: 7.1 g | Protein: 25.2 g |
| Fat: 17.1 g | Fiber: 1.2 g | Net Carbs: 5.9 g |

SUNDAY POT ROAST

SERVES 6

PREP TIME: 5M

COOK TIME: 1H 5M

TOTAL TIME: 1H 10M

1 pound (454 g) radishes,
    rinsed and trimmed

2 cups (480 ml) beef broth

2 bay leaves

2 pounds (908 g) chuck
    roast

2 tablespoons (6 g)
    dried onion

2 teaspoons garlic powder

2 teaspoons salt

1 teaspoon black pepper

4 tablespoons (56 g)
    butter

Pot roast is one of those meals that always satisfies. Serve it to company or deliver it to your bestie. In this recipe, I omitted the prepackaged soup mix and replaced it with clean spices. Potatoes are replaced with radishes, but after a little time in the Instant Pot, you'd never know the difference!

Place the radishes in the pot and cover with the broth. Add the bay leaves.

Place the roast on top of the radishes. Sprinkle the dried onion, garlic powder, salt, and pepper on top of the roast. Top with the butter.

Close the lid and seal the vent. Cook on HIGH pressure for 50 minutes. Let the steam naturally release for 15 minutes before manually releasing.

Carefully remove the roast and place it on a cutting board. Use two forks to shred the meat. Serve with the radishes.

Optional: Use the broth to make gravy by bringing the broth to a boil and whisking in 1 to 1½ teaspoons xanthan gum. (This is not calculated in the macros.)

Note: If desired, add 1 pound (454 g) carrots, halved and trimmed, to the roast. Place them in the pot with the radishes.

Complete the Meal: Creamed Spinach (page 157)
Broccoli with Garlic-Herb Cheese Sauce (page 158)

MACRONUTRIENTS:

| Calories: 492 | Carbs: 4.9 g | Protein: 27.2 g |
| Fat: 39.4 g | Fiber: 1.4 g | Net Carbs: 3.5 g |

CHAPTER 8

Poultry, Pork, and Seafood

Chicken, pork, and seafood may be lean sources of protein, but they're fierce competitors for your Instant Pot! Though they're lower in fat, chicken, pork, and seafood make excellent choices when following a ketogenic diet. With the right pairings, they can provide a plentiful amount of healthy fat and protein. This chapter is full of recipes that are foolproof for those times you need a break from red meat.

SHREDDED CHICKEN

YIELD: 3 CUPS (420 G)

PREP TIME: 5M

COOK TIME: 15M

TOTAL TIME: 20M

1 cup (240 ml) water

2 pounds (908 g) boneless skinless chicken breasts (about 4 large pieces)

2 teaspoons salt

1 teaspoon black pepper

½ teaspoon garlic powder

¼ teaspoon dried thyme

¼ teaspoon ground sage

2 ribs celery, cut in half

½ onion, quartered

2 bay leaves

Something I learned early on in my parenting days was the blessing that is keeping my fridge and freezer stocked with cooked meat. Some days we just don't have the time, energy, or free hands to cook a big fancy meal. Shredded chicken can be used in casseroles, in wraps, salads, tacos, on pizzas . . . the list goes on and on. Having precooked chicken on hand guarantees you can throw together a meal on the craziest of days.

Add the water to the pot and lay the chicken breasts inside.

In a small bowl, combine the salt, pepper, garlic powder, thyme, and sage. Sprinkle on top of the chicken, making sure to coat each piece thoroughly.

Add the celery and onion to the pot, placing them around the sides of the chicken. Place the bay leaves on top of the chicken.

Close the lid and seal the vent. Cook on HIGH pressure for 15 minutes. Quick release the steam.

Remove the chicken from the pot and shred with two forks.

Note: You may also use frozen chicken. Follow the same instructions, but cook for 20 minutes on HIGH pressure and quick release the steam.

ROAST CHICKEN

SERVES 6

PREP TIME: 5M

COOK TIME: 35M

TOTAL TIME: 40M

2 tablespoons (28 g) butter, softened

2 cloves garlic, minced

1½ teaspoons salt

½ teaspoon black pepper

1 whole chicken (4 to 5 pounds, or 1.8 to 2.3 kg)

1 cup (240 ml) water or chicken broth

½ onion, quartered

ACCESSORY NEEDED:

Trivet

Roast chicken is one of the easiest and most versatile recipes a home cook can master. Knowing how to make a whole chicken can save you when unexpected company arrives or you're simply trying to prepare for a busy week. The meat will fall off the bones after a stint in your Instant Pot, so you needn't worry about dried-out chicken. You can save the meat to use in any recipes that call for cooked chicken, or serve the chicken on a big platter for a family dinner.

In a small bowl, combine the butter, garlic, salt, and pepper.

Pat the chicken dry with paper towels. Rub the top of the bird with the butter mixture, making sure to evenly coat the skin.

Add the water or broth to the pot. Place the trivet inside and put the bird on top of the trivet. Add the onion around the edges of the pot.

Close the lid and seal the vent. Cook on HIGH pressure for 30 minutes. Quick release the steam.

Heat the broiler. Remove the chicken from the pot and place on a baking sheet. Place the chicken under the broiler for about 5 minutes to crisp up the skin. Rotate the chicken as needed to ensure even browning.

Complete the Meal: Broccoli with Garlic-Herb Cheese Sauce (page 158)
Sweet Country Carrots (page 171)
Faux Mac and Cheese (page 161)

Note: Macros are approximations, as the edible portion of meat per bird will vary. To ensure accuracy, weigh the meat before consumption and use a fitness app to calculate the nutritional information.

MACRONUTRIENTS FOR A 4-POUND (1.8 KG) CHICKEN:

Calories: 319	Carbs: 0.3 g	Protein: 25.8 g
Fat: 24 g	Fiber: 0 g	Net Carbs: 0.3 g

ANYTIME THANKSGIVING TURKEY

SERVES 8

PREP TIME: 5M

COOK TIME: 60M

TOTAL TIME: 1H 5M

1 turkey breast (7 pounds, or 3.2 kg), giblets removed

4 tablespoons (56 g) butter, softened

2 teaspoons ground sage

2 teaspoons garlic powder

2 teaspoons salt

2 teaspoons black pepper

½ onion, quartered

1 rib celery, cut into 3 or 4 pieces

1 cup (240 ml) chicken broth

2 or 3 bay leaves

1 teaspoon xanthan gum

ACCESSORY NEEDED:

Trivet

Thanksgiving is my all-time favorite holiday. The food, oh, the food! I love cooking in the kitchen with my mom and Gran, prepping the pies and dressing to carry to my aunt's house. I love it so much that a couple of times throughout the year I like to fix a big Thanksgiving dinner. Cooking a Thanksgiving turkey in your Instant Pot is a total game changer! You don't have to baste the bird, and the steam keeps the meat incredibly juicy. Go ahead and fix yourself a Thanksgiving meal on a Tuesday in March!

Pat the turkey dry with a paper towel.

In a small bowl, combine the butter with the sage, garlic powder, salt, and pepper. Rub the butter mixture all over the top of the bird. Place the onion and celery inside the cavity.

Place the trivet in the pot. Add the broth and bay leaves to the pot.

Place the turkey on the trivet. If you need to remove the trivet to make the turkey fit, you can. The turkey will be near the top of the pot, which is fine.

Close the lid and seal the vent. Cook on HIGH pressure for 35 minutes. It is normal if it takes your pot a longer time to come to pressure.

Let the steam naturally release for 20 minutes before manually releasing. Press CANCEL.

Heat the broiler.

Carefully remove the turkey to a sheet pan. Place under the broiler for 5 to 10 minutes to crisp up the skin.

While the skin is crisping, use the juices to make a gravy. Pour the juices through a mesh sieve, reserving 2 cups (480 ml) of broth. Return the reserved broth to the pot. Turn the pot to SAUTÉ mode. When the broth starts to boil, add the xanthan gum and whisk until the desired consistency is reached. Add more xanthan gum if you like a thicker gravy.

Remove the turkey from the broiler and place on a platter. Carve as desired and serve with the gravy.

Complete the Meal: Southern "Corn Bread" Dressing (page 166)
Sweet Country Carrots (page 171)
Horseradish Whipped Cauliflower (page 162)

Note: Macros are approximations, as the edible portion of meat per bird will vary. To ensure accuracy, weigh the meat before consumption and use a fitness app to calculate the nutritional information.

MACRONUTRIENTS:

Calories: 380	Carbs: 2.5 g	Protein: 47.1 g
Fat: 18.3 g	Fiber: 1.9 g	Net Carbs: 0.6 g

BACON AND CREAM CHEESE–STUFFED CHICKEN WITH BACON GRAVY

SERVES 4

PREP TIME: 10M

COOK TIME: 13M

TOTAL TIME: 23M

4 boneless, skinless chicken breasts (about 2 pounds, or 1816 kg)

6 ounces (168 g) cream cheese, softened

3 pieces cooked bacon, chopped (about ¾ cup, or 60 g), divided

2 tablespoons (10 g) grated Parmesan cheese

1 teaspoon bacon grease

¼ teaspoon garlic powder

½ cup (120 ml) water

¼ cup (60 ml) half-and-half

ACCESSORY NEEDED:

Trivet

This recipe is near and dear to my heart. I adapted the most popular recipe on my blog for the Instant Pot. But honestly, can you go wrong with bacon gravy? The next time you need to wow someone with your cooking, this recipe is a sure bet!

Make a small slit in the side of the chicken breasts to create a pocket for the filling.

In a small bowl, combine the cream cheese, ½ cup (40 g) of the bacon pieces, Parmesan, bacon grease, and garlic powder.

Stuff each chicken breast with 2 tablespoons (30 g) of the cream cheese mixture. Use toothpicks to seal the chicken. You will have some cheese mixture left over.

Place the chicken on a piece of aluminum foil and wrap the sides up around it to create a packet. Do not cover the tops of the chicken.

Place the trivet in the pot and add the water. Place the foil packet on top of the trivet.

Close the lid and seal the vent. Cook on HIGH pressure for 10 minutes. Quick release the steam.

Remove the chicken from the pot and drain the water.

Turn the pot to SAUTÉ mode. Add the remaining cheese mixture and the half-and-half. Stir until melted and a sauce has formed, about 3 minutes.

Remove the toothpicks from the chicken. Top each breast with 2 tablespoons (30 ml) of sauce. Sprinkle with the remaining bacon crumbles.

Note: You may make the sauce in a nonstick skillet on the stovetop to have it ready for when the chicken is finished.

MACRONUTRIENTS:

Calories: 386	Carbs: 2.2 g	Protein 39.7 g
Fat: 23.8 g	Fiber: 0 g	Net Carbs: 2.2 g

CHICKEN WITH SPINACH AND SUN-DRIED TOMATOES

SERVES 4

PREP TIME: 5M

COOK TIME: 18M

TOTAL TIME: 23M

4 boneless, skinless chicken breasts (about 2 pounds, or 1816 g)

2½ ounces (70 g) sun-dried tomatoes, coarsely chopped (about 2 tablespoons)

¼ cup (60 ml) chicken broth

2 tablespoons (30 ml) creamy, no-sugar-added balsamic vinegar dressing

1 tablespoon (11 g) whole-grain mustard

2 cloves garlic, minced

1 teaspoon salt

8 ounces (227 g) fresh spinach

¼ cup (60 g) sour cream

1 ounce (28 g) cream cheese, softened

If you want to impress your non-keto friends with a keto recipe, this is the one to use! A decadent cream sauce is infused with sundried tomatoes, garlic, and spinach. It's delicious on its own, or you can serve it on top of a bed of Homemade Egg Noodles (page 19) or spaghetti squash. Pair it with a simple Caesar salad for a robust keto supper.

Place the chicken breasts in the Instant Pot. Add the tomatoes, broth, and dressing.

Close the lid and seal the vent. Cook on HIGH pressure for 10 minutes. Quick release the steam. Press CANCEL.

Remove the chicken from the pot and place on a plate. Cover with aluminum foil to keep warm while you make the sauce.

Turn the pot to SAUTÉ mode. Whisk in the mustard, garlic, and salt and then add the spinach. Stir the spinach continuously until it is completely cooked down, 2 to 3 minutes. The spinach will absorb the sauce but will release it again as it continues to cook down.

Once the spinach is completely wilted, add the sour cream and cream cheese. Whisk until completed incorporated.

Let the sauce simmer to thicken and reduce by about one-third, about 5 minutes. Stir occasionally to prevent burning. Press CANCEL.

Pour the sauce over the chicken.

MACRONUTRIENTS:

Calories: 357	Carbs: 6.7 g	Protein: 52.5 g
Fat: 13.1 g	Fiber: 1.4 g	Net Carbs: 5.3 g

CHICKEN FAJITAS

SERVES 4

PREP TIME: 10M

COOK TIME: 5M

TOTAL TIME: 15M

1½ pounds (680 g) boneless, skinless chicken breasts

¼ cup (60 ml) avocado oil

2 tablespoons (30 ml) water

1 tablespoon (15 ml) Mexican hot sauce

2 cloves garlic, minced

1 teaspoon lime juice

1 teaspoon ground cumin

1 teaspoon salt

1 teaspoon erythritol

¼ teaspoon chili powder

¼ teaspoon smoked paprika

5 ounces (140 g) sliced yellow bell pepper strips

5 ounces (140 g) sliced red bell pepper strips

5 ounces (140 g) sliced green bell pepper strips

If you're like me, then tacos aren't reserved for Tuesdays. My family loves taco night, and I always oblige because they're affordable and easy-peasy to whip up! Everyone enjoys building their own tacos, and I like encouraging their creativity in the kitchen. These fajitas are a breeze to make in the Instant Pot and much faster to prepare on a busy night. Serve them with Mexican Cauliflower Rice (page 20), radish chips, and all the taco bar fixin's!

Slice the chicken into very thin strips lengthwise. Cut each strip in half again. Imagine the thickness of restaurant fajitas when cutting.

In a measuring cup, whisk together the avocado oil, water, hot sauce, garlic, lime juice, cumin, salt, erythritol, chili powder, and paprika to form a marinade. Add to the pot, along with the chicken and peppers.

Close the lid and seal the vent. Cook on HIGH pressure for 5 minutes. Quick release the steam.

MACRONUTRIENTS:

| Calories: 319 | Carbs: 5.5 g | Protein: 34 g |
| Fat: 18.7 g | Fiber: 1.8 g | Net Carbs: 3.7 g |

GOAT CHEESE AND BRUSCHETTA–STUFFED CHICKEN

SERVES 4

PREP TIME: 10M

COOK TIME: 10M

TOTAL TIME: 20M

6 ounces (168 g) diced Roma tomatoes

2 tablespoons (30 ml) avocado oil

1 tablespoon (2.5 g) thinly sliced fresh basil, plus more for garnish

1½ teaspoons balsamic vinegar

Pinch of salt

Pinch of black pepper

4 boneless, skinless chicken breasts (about 2 pounds, or 1816 g)

12 ounces (340 g) goat cheese, divided

2 teaspoons Italian seasoning, divided

1 cup (240 ml) water

ACCESSORY NEEDED:

Trivet

This chicken is a mouthwatering way to satisfy your cravings for Italian food. Pairing tangy goat cheese with sweet bruschetta is a delicious way to turn a boring chicken breast into an elegant meal. The goat cheese melts into a creamy filling in the chicken while the bruschetta keeps the dish light and crisp. Serve the chicken alongside a Caesar salad for a *pasto completo*!

Prepare the bruschetta by mixing the tomatoes, avocado oil, basil, vinegar, salt, and pepper in a small bowl. Let it marinate until the chicken is done.

Pat the chicken dry with a paper towel. Butterfly the breast open but do not cut all the way through. Stuff each breast with 3 ounces (84 g) of the goat cheese. Use toothpicks to close the edges.

Sprinkle ½ teaspoon of the Italian seasoning on top of each breast.

Pour the water into the pot. Place the trivet inside. Lay a piece of aluminum foil on top of the trivet and place the chicken breasts on top. It is okay if they overlap.

Close the lid and seal the vent. Cook on HIGH pressure for 10 minutes. Quick release the steam.

Remove the toothpicks and top each breast with one-fourth of the bruschetta.

Complete the Meal: Rosemary Mushrooms (page 163)
Creamed Spinach (page 157)

MACRONUTRIENTS:

| Calories: 581 | Carbs: 4.8 g | Protein: 63.9 g |
| Fat: 33.9 g | Fiber: 1 g | Net Carbs: 3.8 g |

CHILI-LIME TURKEY BURGERS WITH SRIRACHA-LIME DIPPING SAUCE

SERVES 4

PREP TIME: 10M

COOK TIME: 3M

TOTAL TIME: 13M

FOR BURGERS:

2 pounds (1816 g) ground turkey

1½ ounces (42 g) diced red onion

2 cloves garlic, minced

1½ teaspoons minced cilantro

1½ teaspoons salt

1 teaspoon Mexican chili powder

Juice and zest of 1 lime

½ cup (120 ml) water

FOR DIPPING SAUCE:

½ cup (120 g) sour cream

4 teaspoons (20 ml) sriracha

1 tablespoon (1 g) chopped cilantro, plus more for garnish

1 teaspoon lime juice

ACCESSORY NEEDED:

Trivet

These burgers were inspired by the premade burgers from the Trader Joe's grocery store. Living in a small town in Kentucky, we don't have a TJ's anywhere near us, and I am always envious of my friends who get to buy their delicious keto-friendly foods. These turkey burgers cook insanely fast and pack a punch of citrus and heat. Top them with a slice of Monterey Jack cheese and my dipping sauce for a twist on the bunless burger!

To make the burgers: In a large bowl, add the turkey, onion, garlic, cilantro, salt, chili powder, and lime juice and zest. Use a wooden spoon to mix until the ingredients are well distributed.

Divide the meat into four 8-ounce (227 g) balls. Use a kitchen scale to measure for accuracy. Pat the meat into thick patties, about 1" (2.5 cm) thick.

Add the water and trivet to the Instant Pot. Place the turkey patties on top of the trivet, overlapping if necessary.

Close the lid and seal the vent. Cook on HIGH pressure for 3 minutes. Quick release the steam.

Remove the patties from the pot.

To make the dipping sauce: In a small bowl, whisk together the sour cream, sriracha, cilantro, and lime juice.

Top each patty with 2 tablespoons (30 ml) of the sauce and garnish with fresh cilantro.

MACRONUTRIENTS:

Calories: 417	Carbs: 4.8 g	Protein: 43.7 g
Fat: 25.1 g	Fiber: 0.5 g	Net Carbs: 4.3 g

COD FILLETS WITH BASIL BUTTER

SERVES 4

PREP TIME: 5M

COOK TIME: 12M

TOTAL TIME: 17M

½ cup (120 ml) water

4 frozen cod fillets
(about 6 ounces,
or 168 g, each)

1 teaspoon dried basil

Pinch of salt

Pinch of black pepper

4 lemon slices

¼ cup (60 ml) heavy
cream

2 tablespoons (28 g)
butter, softened

1 ounce (28 g) cream
cheese, softened

2 teaspoons lemon juice

1½ teaspoons chopped
fresh basil, plus more
for garnish (optional)

Lemon wedges, for
garnish (optional)

ACCESSORY NEEDED:

Trivet

One of the appealing features of the Instant Pot is its ability to cook foods from frozen in a flash without overcooking them. Frozen fish fillets are economical and easy for a busy weeknight meal. This dish tastes like a restaurant-quality meal and is ready in less than half an hour.

Place the trivet inside the pot and add the water. Lay a piece of aluminum foil on top of the trivet and place the cod on top.

Sprinkle the fish with the dried basil, salt, and pepper. Set a lemon slice on top of each fillet.

Close the lid and seal the vent. Cook on HIGH pressure for 9 minutes. Quick release the steam. Press CANCEL.

Remove the trivet and fish from the pot. Rinse the pot if needed and turn to SAUTÉ mode.

Add the cream and butter and whisk as the butter melts and the cream warms up. Add the cream cheese and whisk until thickened, 2 to 3 minutes. Add the lemon juice and another pinch of salt and pepper. Once the sauce is thickened and well combined, 1 to 2 minutes, press CANCEL and add the fresh basil.

Pour the sauce over the fish. Garnish with fresh basil or a lemon wedge, if desired.

Note: If your cod fillets aren't frozen, reduce the cook time to 4 minutes.

MACRONUTRIENTS:

Calories: 221	Carbs: 0.7 g	Protein: 26.6 g
Fat: 11.3 g	Fiber: 0 g	Net Carbs: 0.7 g

EASY LOBSTER TAILS

SERVES 2

PREP TIME: 5M

COOK TIME: 3M

TOTAL TIME: 8M

2 fresh (or thawed) lobster tails, about 4 ounces (112 g) each

1 cup (240 ml) water

ACCESSORY NEEDED:

Trivet

I used to save lobster tails for nights of fine dining or Caribbean vacations, but those times are few and far between these days. Believe it or not, cooking a lobster tail is very simple, especially when you use your Instant Pot. Similar to the No-Boil Crab Legs on page 136, they cook quickly without any fuss. The next time you want to impress someone with a fancy meal, "lobstah" (and you must say it like that) is the way to go. Don't forget the melted butter for dipping!

Prepare the lobster tails by placing them flat-side down on a cutting board. Using kitchen shears, cut open the top of the shell all the way to the bottom. Use your hands to butterfly, or push open, the shell to expose the meat. This will allow the meat to cook up and out of the shell.

Pour the water into the pot and place the trivet inside. Set the lobster tails on top of the trivet, flat-side down.

Close the lid and seal the vent. Cook on STEAM mode for 3 minutes. Quick release the steam.

Complete the Meal: Beef Tenderloin with Red Wine Reduction (page 99) Horseradish Whipped Cauliflower (page 162)

Note: Macros are approximations, as the edible portion of meat per tail will vary. To ensure accuracy, weigh the meat before consumption and use a fitness app to calculate the nutritional information. If you do not have the STEAM setting on your pot, use HIGH pressure for the same amount of time.

MACRONUTRIENTS:

Calories: 87	Carbs: 0 g	Protein: 19 g
Fat: 0.9 g	Fiber: 0 g	Net Carbs: 0 g

COFFEE-RUBBED PULLED PORK

SERVES 10

PREP TIME: 10M

COOK TIME: 1H 30M

TOTAL TIME: 1H 40M

2 tablespoons (12 g) ground coffee

2 tablespoons (32 g) brown sugar substitute

2 tablespoons (12 g) chili powder

1 tablespoon (18 g) salt

1 tablespoon (6 g) black pepper

1 tablespoon (7 g) onion powder

1 tablespoon (7 g) smoked paprika

2 teaspoons garlic powder

2 teaspoons ground mustard

4 to 5 pounds (1.8 to 2.3 kg) pork shoulder (Boston butt)

1 cup (240 ml) beef broth

I love the diversity of BBQ across the United States. Where I come from, BBQ is almost a religion. This recipe for pulled pork is much easier than standing around a smoker all day and leaves you with flavorful and tender meat. You can use it in salads, atop a sweet potato (if you like to carb up), or all on its own. You can also use the leftover pulled pork in my Georgia Brunswick Stew (page 73).

Prepare the rub by combining the coffee, brown sugar substitute, and all the spices in a bowl. Use a fork to mix them together until well combined.

Pat the meat dry with a paper towel so the rub will adhere to it. If your meat is too large to fit in your Instant Pot, cut it into two or three pieces.

Coat every side of the meat with the rub. Be liberal with the rub and massage it into the meat. Don't be afraid to get your hands dirty! Be sure to use ALL of the rub.

Pour the broth into the pot. Place the meat into the pot.

Close the lid and seal the vent. Cook on HIGH pressure for 90 minutes. Quick release the steam.

Remove the meat from the pot and place it on a cutting board. Shred the meat with two forks. It should fall apart very easily.

Optional: Strain the juices in the pot and save for dipping the meat into. You can also save some of the juices for pouring on top of leftover meat to keep it moist in the refrigerator.

Note: Make a batch of my homemade BBQ sauce on page 95 for your pulled pork!

Complete the Meal: Southern-Style Green Beans (page 167)
Maple Bacon Corn Bread (page 165)
Twice-Baked Mashed Cauliflower (page 173)

MACRONUTRIENTS:

Calories: 387	Carbs: 1.8 g	Protein: 36.4 g
Fat: 25.2 g	Fiber: 0.3 g	Net Carbs: 1.5 g

CRISPY CHICKEN THIGHS WITH GRAVY

SERVES 4

PREP TIME: 5M

COOK TIME: 28M

TOTAL TIME: 33M

8 bone-in, skin-on chicken thighs

1½ teaspoons salt, divided

1 teaspoon garlic powder

1 teaspoon paprika

1 teaspoon black pepper

2 tablespoons (30 ml) avocado oil

½ cup (120 ml) water

6 tablespoons (90 ml) heavy cream

1 teaspoon brown sugar substitute

1 teaspoon xanthan gum

ACCESSORY NEEDED:

Trivet

Chicken and gravy go together like two peas in a pod. One of the reasons keto is so easy for me to stick to is because I get to eat meals like this one. My southern heart would not do well if I had to live in a world without gravy. Thankfully, this no-fuss recipe makes sure I never have to!

Pat the chicken thighs dry with a paper towel.

In a small bowl, combine 1 teaspoon of the salt, the garlic powder, paprika, and pepper to make a rub. Sprinkle the rub on each side of the chicken thighs and rub into the skin.

Turn the pot to SAUTÉ mode and add the avocado oil. Once hot, sear the thighs, four at a time, skin-side down, until the skin easily loosens from the pot, about 5 minutes. Remove to a plate and sear the four remaining thighs. Transfer to a plate when completed. Press CANCEL.

Add the water to the pot. Place the trivet inside. Layer the thighs on top of the trivet, overlapping or stacking if necessary.

Close the lid and seal the vent. Cook on HIGH pressure for 10 minutes. Quick release the steam. Press CANCEL.

Heat the broiler. Remove the chicken thighs to a baking sheet. Broil until the skin is crispy, about 5 minutes.

Turn the pot to SAUTÉ mode. Add the cream, brown sugar substitute, and remaining ½ teaspoon salt. Whisk continuously so the cream doesn't burn. When the mixture begins to bubble, add the xanthan gum and continue whisking until the gravy reaches the desired consistency, about 3 minutes.

Note: Add mushrooms or onions to the pot to cook with the chicken for a little extra pizzazz.

Note: Due to the weight difference of chicken thighs, macros are approximate.

MACRONUTRIENTS:

Calories: 585   Carbs: 5.4 g   Protein: 57 g
Fat: 15.4 g   Fiber: 3.7 g   Net Carbs: 1.7 g

GREEK CHICKEN

SERVES 4

PREP TIME: 5M

COOK TIME: 15M

TOTAL TIME: 20M

1 cup (240 ml) no-sugar-
added Greek salad
dressing

1 can (6 ounces, or 168 g)
black olives, drained

4½ ounces (126 g) cherry
tomatoes

2 ounces (56 g) diced
red onion

4 boneless, skinless
chicken breasts (about
2 pounds, or 1816 g)

½ teaspoon dried dill

½ teaspoon dried
rosemary

½ teaspoon dried oregano

½ teaspoon salt

½ cup (120 g) sour cream

3 ounces (84 g) feta
cheese

2 ounces (56 g) diced
cucumber (optional)

Mediterranean food exudes health and wellness. It's fresh,
clean, and simple. This Greek Chicken was inspired by the
Mediterranean culture. The recipe is full of healthy fat and
protein without being heavy on the palate. Serve alongside a
big Greek salad for a full meal.

Add the salad dressing, olives, tomatoes, and onion to the pot. Place
the chicken breasts on top and season with the dill, rosemary, oregano,
and salt.

Close the lid and seal the vent. Cook on HIGH pressure for 15 minutes.
Quick release the steam.

Remove the chicken from the pot and place on a platter. Use a slotted
spoon to remove the olives, tomatoes, and onion. Place them on the
platter with the chicken. Pour the marinade into a bowl or glass measuring
cup and reserve ½ cup (120 ml).

In a small bowl, combine the reserved marinade and sour cream, mixing
until thoroughly combined.

Drizzle the sauce on top of the chicken. Top with the feta cheese and
cucumber, if using. You may also garnish with extra red onion, if desired.
(Extra red onion and cucumbers are not included in the macros.)

MACRONUTRIENTS:

Calories: 713	Carbs: 8.4 g	Protein: 54.2 g
Fat: 50.1 g	Fiber: 1.9 g	Net Carbs: 6.5 g

HOLIDAY SPIRAL HAM

SERVES 6

PREP TIME: 5M

COOK TIME: 17M

TOTAL TIME: 22M

⅓ cup (80 ml) sugar-free maple syrup

2 tablespoons (32 g) brown sugar substitute

1 tablespoon (15 ml) + 1 cup (240 ml) water, divided

½ teaspoon allspice

Pinch of salt

1 boneless spiral ham (3 to 4 pounds, or 1.4 to 1.8 kg)

¾ teaspoon xanthan gum

ACCESSORIES NEEDED:

7" (18 cm) baking dish

Trivet

When it comes to the holidays, I am Team Ham all the way. The honey-baked variety is my absolute favorite, and there were many a year when my mom would wait in a very long line to make sure we had one for Christmas and Easter. That's a mother's love! I put a keto twist on the traditional sweet honey ham so that you can continue the tradition with your own family. Sometimes I even like to add a bit of orange extract for a pop of citrus!

In a small bowl, whisk together the maple syrup, brown sugar substitute, 1 tablespoon (15 ml) of the water, allspice, and salt.

Place the ham inside the baking dish and loosen the slices of ham. Drizzle the syrup mixture on top of the ham slices. Be sure to work the mixture in between each slice of ham.

Add the remaining 1 cup (240 ml) water to the pot and place the trivet inside. Place the baking dish with the ham on top of the trivet.

Close the lid and seal the vent. Cook on LOW pressure for 15 minutes. Quick release the steam.

Use the handles on the trivet to carefully remove the baking dish and trivet from the pot. Drain the water from the pot. Press CANCEL.

Pour the juices that have gathered in the baking dish into the pot. Turn the pot to SAUTÉ mode. Let the juices begin to heat up and add the xanthan gum. Whisk until a thick and sticky glaze is achieved, 1 to 2 minutes. Pour the glaze on top of the ham before serving.

Complete the Meal: Faux Mac and Cheese (page 161)
Southern-Style Green Beans (page 167)

MACRONUTRIENTS PER SERVING FOR 3 POUNDS (1.4 KG) HAM + GLAZE:

Calories: 135

Fat: 3 g

Carbs: 3.8 g

Fiber: 1.8 g

Protein: 20 g

Net Carbs: 3 g

LEMON CHICKEN

SERVES 4
PREP TIME: 5M
COOK TIME: 15M
TOTAL TIME: 20M

½ cup (120 ml) chicken broth

4 boneless, skinless chicken breasts (about 2 pounds, or 1816 g)

1 teaspoon dried parsley

¼ teaspoon paprika

¼ teaspoon salt

Pinch of black pepper

4 lemon slices

3 cloves garlic, smashed

3 tablespoons (45 g) heavy cream

3 ounces (84 g) cream cheese, softened

⅓ cup (35 g) grated Parmesan cheese

Lemon wedges, for garnish

ACCESSORY NEEDED:

Trivet

My husband and I love to watch reruns of a TV show from the late '90s in which the mom is a terrible cook and one of the only recipes she can fix is dry lemon chicken. We had a good laugh when I told my husband I was including lemon chicken in this cookbook. Thankfully, this recipe is a far cry from the character's. Juicy chicken breasts are infused with lemon and topped with a creamy lemon sauce in this Instant Pot version.

Add the broth to the pot. Place the trivet inside. Lay the chicken breasts on top of the trivet.

In a small bowl, mix together the parsley, paprika, salt, and pepper. Sprinkle the mixture evenly on top of the chicken breasts. Lay the lemon slices and smashed garlic on top of the chicken.

Close the lid and seal the vent. Cook on HIGH pressure for 10 minutes. Quick release the steam. Press CANCEL.

Remove the chicken from the pot. Discard the garlic cloves and lemon slices. Reserve ¼ cup (60 ml) of the chicken broth to make the sauce. Strain the broth if necessary.

Turn the pot to SAUTÉ mode. Add the broth and cream. When the mixture begins to bubble along the edges, add the cream cheese. Whisk as the cream cheese melts and the sauce thickens, about 5 minutes. Press CANCEL. Whisk in the Parmesan. Pour the sauce over the chicken and garnish with a lemon wedge.

MACRONUTRIENTS:

Calories: 384	Carbs: 1.6 g	Protein: 54.4 g
Fat: 16.8 g	Fiber: 0.1 g	Net Carbs: 1.5 g

MAPLE-BOURBON SALMON

SERVES 4

PREP TIME: 5M

COOK TIME: 5M

TOTAL TIME: 10M

½ cup (120 ml) water

¼ cup (60 ml) sugar-free maple syrup

2 tablespoons (30 ml) bourbon or whiskey

1 tablespoon (11 g) Dijon mustard

1 tablespoon (16 g) brown sugar substitute

1½ teaspoons lemon juice

¼ teaspoon orange extract

4 skin-on salmon fillets (5 ounces, or 140 g, each)

Pinch of salt

Pinch of black pepper

1 tablespoon (6 g) arrowroot powder

1 tablespoon (15 ml) water

½ ounce (14 g) pecans, chopped (optional)

ACCESSORY NEEDED:

Trivet

This recipe is going to be your new go-to for all of your salmon cravings! If you don't have bourbon or whiskey, you can substitute chicken or vegetable broth.

Add the water, syrup, bourbon, mustard, brown sugar substitute, lemon juice, and orange extract to the pot and whisk together.

Place the trivet inside the pot. Lay the salmon on top of the trivet, skin-side down.

Sprinkle the salt and pepper on top of the salmon.

Close the lid and seal the vent. Cook on HIGH pressure for 4 minutes. Quick release the steam. Press CANCEL.

Carefully remove the trivet with the salmon from the pot.

In a small bowl, whisk together the arrowroot powder and water to make a slurry.

Turn the pot to SAUTÉ mode. When the mixture starts to bubble, add the slurry and whisk until it has thickened, a few seconds. If adding the pecans, add them in at this step as well, reserving a few for garnish at the end. If your sauce seems too thick, you may thin it out with a little bit of water.

Top each fillet with 2 to 3 tablespoons (30 to 45 ml) of sauce. Garnish with the reserved pecans, if using.

Complete the Meal: Creamed Spinach (page 157)
Horseradish Whipped Cauliflower (page 162)

MACRONUTRIENTS:

Calories: 255	Carbs: 15.7 g	Protein: 30 g
Fat: 8.5 g	Fiber: 11.4 g	Net Carbs: 4.3 g

NO-BOIL CRAB LEGS

SERVES 2

PREP TIME: 5M

COOK TIME: 3M

TOTAL TIME: 8M

1 pound (454 g) king
    crab legs (about
    2 large legs)
1 cup (240 ml) water

ACCESSORY NEEDED:

Steamer basket

Crab legs are such a treat whenever I'm able to get my hands on them. Growing up, we had them every New Year's Eve, and my momma would even crack the shells for us. My, how times have changed! I love using my Instant Pot to quickly prepare crab legs—any time of year. Save time waiting for water to boil (and subsequently spilling it all over the stove). Don't forget to serve it with a little melted butter for dipping.

Prepare the crab legs for cooking by breaking them at the joints to separate the legs into smaller pieces. If necessary, use kitchen shears to cut them into smaller sections.

Pour the water into the pot. Place the crab legs in the steamer basket and into the pot. Make sure that the legs are not sticking out over the inner pot.

Close the lid and seal the vent. Cook on STEAM mode for 3 minutes. Quick release the steam.

Complete the Meal: Twice-Baked Mashed Cauliflower (page 173)
Classic Cheesecake (page 182)

Note: Macros are approximations, as the edible portion of meat per leg will vary. To ensure accuracy, weigh the meat before consumption and use a fitness app to calculate the nutritional information. If you do not have the STEAM setting on your pot, use HIGH pressure for the same amount of time.

MACRONUTRIENTS:

Calories: 309	Carbs: 0 g	Protein: 67.4 g
Fat: 2.2 g	Fiber: 0 g	Net Carbs: 0 g

PIMENTO CHEESE CRACK CHICKEN

SERVES 6

PREP TIME: 5M

COOK TIME: 5M

TOTAL TIME: 10M

½ cup (120 ml) water

2 cups (280 g) cooked chicken or Roast Chicken (page 115)

1 packet (1 ounce, or 28 g) dry ranch mix

1 cup (240 g) Pimento Cheese Dip (page 55), not melted

4 ounces (112 g) cream cheese, softened and cut into cubes

Bacon bits (optional)

Shredded Cheddar cheese (optional)

"Crack chicken" is one of my family's favorite weeknight meals. It's incredibly simple, yet super tasty. This pimento cheese version is a jazzed-up Southern variation of the original. If you don't have a batch of the Pimento Cheese Dip (page 55) made, make half a batch for this recipe.

Add the water to the pot. Place the chicken inside and sprinkle the ranch mix on top of the chicken.

Add the cold pimento cheese dip and cream cheese to the top of the chicken. Do not stir.

Close the lid and seal the vent. Cook on HIGH pressure for 5 minutes. Quick release the steam.

Open the lid and stir the mixture until it is well combined.

Top each serving with bacon bits and shredded Cheddar cheese, if desired. (These are not calculated in the macros.)

MACRONUTRIENTS:

Calories: 299.5

Fat: 22.3 g

Carbs: 1.6 g

Fiber: 0.3 g

Protein: 22.9 g

Net Carbs: 1.3 g

PORK CHOPS WITH MAPLE-DIJON CREAM SAUCE

SERVES 6

PREP TIME: 5M

COOK TIME: 15M

TOTAL TIME: 20M

6 thick-cut boneless pork chops (about 2½ pounds, or 1135 g)

1 cup (240 ml) chicken broth

¼ cup (60 ml) sugar-free maple syrup

2 tablespoons (22 g) Dijon mustard

1 teaspoon apple cider vinegar

Pinch of salt

8 ounces (227 g) sliced baby bella mushrooms

4 ounces (112 g) thinly sliced onion (about ½ onion)

⅓ cup (80 ml) heavy cream

1½ teaspoons xanthan gum

The Instant Pot isn't just for soups and tough cuts of meat. Tender and lean meats such as pork chops can be made quickly and effortlessly. These pork chops stay juicy without shredding like pulled pork. Top them with a creamy maple-Dijon sauce to amp up the fat. This recipe is a pleasing dish that your family is sure to love!

Place the pork chops in the pot. They may overlap, if necessary.

In a large measuring cup, whisk together the broth, syrup, mustard, vinegar, and salt.

Pour the broth mixture on top of the pork chops. Add the mushrooms and onion to the pot.

Close the lid and seal the vent. Cook on HIGH pressure for 10 minutes. Quick release the steam. Press CANCEL.

Remove the pork chops and transfer to a plate. Use a slotted spoon to remove the mushrooms and onions from the juices and put them on the plate with the pork chops. Cover the plate with aluminum foil to keep warm.

Turn the pot to SAUTÉ mode. Add the cream and xanthan gum to the broth. Whisk continuously as the sauce begins to bubble and thicken. Let the sauce cook until the desired consistency is reached, 3 to 5 minutes.

Pour the sauce on top of the pork chops before serving.

Complete the Meal: Twice-Baked Mashed Cauliflower (page 173) Southern-Style Green Beans (page 167)

MACRONUTRIENTS:

Calories: 490	Carbs: 10.5 g	Protein: 40 g
Fat: 32.9 g	Fiber: 6.7 g	Net Carbs: 3.8 g

PORK TENDERLOIN MEDALLIONS WITH PAN SAUCE

SERVES 6

PREP TIME: 5M

COOK TIME: 12M

TOTAL TIME: 17M

2 pounds (908 g) pork
    tenderloin

1 tablespoon (11 g) Dijon
    mustard

2 tablespoons (32 g)
    brown sugar substitute

1 tablespoon (4 g) minced
    fresh parsley

1 clove garlic, minced

1½ teaspoons avocado oil

¼ cup (60 ml) water

½ teaspoon apple
    cider vinegar

¼ teaspoon xanthan gum

ACCESSORY NEEDED:

Trivet

Have you ever made a pork tenderloin only to cut into it and find that it's completely dried out? Well, guess what? Cooking your pork tenderloin in the Instant Pot will guarantee you never have dried-out meat again!

Pat the tenderloin dry with a paper towel. Brush the mustard all over the meat with a pastry brush.

In a small bowl, mix together the brown sugar substitute, parsley, and garlic. Rub the mixture all over the meat.

Turn the pot to SAUTÉ mode. Add the avocado oil. Once hot, sear the tenderloin on all sides. This should take no more than 5 minutes. Press CANCEL. Remove the tenderloin from the pot.

Add the water and the trivet to the pot. Place your tenderloin on the trivet.

Close the lid and seal the vent. Cook on LOW pressure for 2 minutes. Let the steam naturally release for 10 minutes, then release manually. Press CANCEL.

Remove the tenderloin to a platter and cover with aluminum foil. Let rest for 10 minutes while you make the sauce. Remove the trivet.

Turn the pot to SAUTÉ mode. When the juices start to bubble, add the vinegar and xanthan gum. Whisk continuously until the sauce is thickened, 1 to 2 minutes.

Slice the tenderloin crosswise into medallions and drizzle the sauce on top.

Note: This cook time will yield a blush pink center, which is the desired doneness of pork, according to the Ohio Pork Council.

Complete the Meal: Broccoli with Garlic-Herb Cheese Sauce (page 158) Horseradish Whipped Cauliflower (page 162)

MACRONUTRIENTS:

| Calories: 239 | Carbs: 6.4 g | Protein: 41.9 g |
| Fat: 5.8 g | Fiber: 2.7 g | Net Carbs: 3.7 g |

SALSA VERDE CARNITAS

SERVES 6

PREP TIME: 5M

COOK TIME: 60M

TOTAL TIME: 1H 15M

- 12 ounces (340 g) salsa verde
- 1 cup (240 ml) ultra-light beer (or chicken broth)
- 2½ pounds (1135 g) pork shoulder (Boston butt)
- 3 ounces (84 g) chopped onion, (about ½ onion)
- 3 cloves garlic, coarsely chopped
- 1 tablespoon (3 g) dried oregano
- 1 tablespoon (6 g) ground cumin
- 2 teaspoons salt
- ½ teaspoon black pepper

This recipe is a keto spin on a traditional Mexican dish. Carnitas are a Mexican-style pulled pork that's often eaten in a taco or burrito. The beer adds an extra depth of flavor, but if you're sensitive to gluten, swap it for chicken broth. The salsa verde packs a punch of heat, but it's gentle enough for little eaters. Elevate your next taco night with this marvelous and effortless recipe.

Add the salsa verde and beer (or chicken broth) to the pot. Place the pork shoulder inside.

Add the onions, garlic, oregano, cumin, salt, and pepper to the pot.

Close the lid and seal the vent. Cook on HIGH pressure for 60 minutes. Quick release the steam.

Let the meat rest for 10 minutes before shredding with two forks. Use a slotted spoon to scoop some of the onion and garlic salsa from the bottom of the pot and place on top of the meat before serving.

Note: This recipe should yield approximately 1 pound (454 g) of shredded meat when finished.

MACRONUTRIENTS:

Calories: 384	Carbs: 4.9 g	Protein: 32.7 g
Fat: 23 g	Fiber: 0.7 g	Net Carbs: 4.2 g

SALMON FILLETS WITH LEMON-DILL BUTTER

SERVES 4

PREP TIME: 5M

COOK TIME: 3M

TOTAL TIME: 8M

4 salmon fillets (5 to 6 ounces, or 140 to 168 g, each)

4 tablespoons (56 g) butter, softened

1½ teaspoons dried dill

1 teaspoon lemon juice

2 tablespoons (17 g) capers, drained

1 cup (240 ml) water

ACCESSORY NEEDED:

Trivet

We all know salmon is good for our hearts, but did you know it is one of the healthiest sources of fat on a ketogenic diet? Salmon is chock-full of omega-3 fats, which can help lower your triglycerides. Use your Instant Pot to make perfectly flaky fillets in less than 10 minutes—if that's not fast food, I don't know what is! Make a super fast side by steaming broccoli.

Pat the salmon dry with a paper towel. Place the fillets on a large piece of aluminum foil.

In a small bowl, mix together the butter, dill, and lemon juice.

Spread one-fourth of the butter mixture on top of each fillet.

Roll the edges of the foil up toward the fillets to create a foil packet.

Top each fillet with 1½ teaspoons capers. There's no need to seal the foil packets.

Add the water to pot. Place the foil packet on top of the trivet and carefully lower it into the pot.

Close the lid and seal the vent. Cook on STEAM mode for 3 minutes. Quick release the steam. Pour the melted butter left over in the foil packet on top of the fish.

Note: If your Instant Pot does not have the STEAM setting, use HIGH pressure for the same amount of time.

Complete the Meal: Spaghetti Squash Alfredo (page 168)

MACRONUTRIENTS:

Calories: 312	Carbs: 0.5 g	Protein: 39.2 g
Fat: 17.1 g	Fiber: 0.2 g	Net Carbs: 0.3 g

SAUERKRAUT PORK ROAST

SERVES 6

PREP TIME: 5M

COOK TIME: 50M

TOTAL TIME: 1H 5M

½ cup (120 ml) chicken broth

2½ pounds (1135 g) boneless pork loin (not tenderloin)

¼ cup (64 g) brown sugar substitute

1 jar (32 ounces, or 908 g) sauerkraut

The area we live in is heavily influenced by German culture. In fact, we have the second largest Oktoberfest festival in the entire world! Although sauerkraut may be Germany's most famous dish, did you know that it is a superfood for your gut? Be sure to choose the refrigerated fermented cabbage (not canned) because its probiotics help feed your brain, your immune system, and your digestive tract. Not only is it overwhelmingly beneficial for our health, it also tastes fantastic! Sauerkraut has a pickly-tangy taste that pairs excellently with pork.

Add the broth to the pot. Place the pork inside, fat-side down.

Press the brown sugar substitute onto the top of the roast.

Pour the jar of sauerkraut on top of and around the pork.

Close the lid and seal the vent. Cook on HIGH pressure for 50 minutes. Quick release the steam.

Remove the pork to a platter. Use a spoon to transfer the sauerkraut from the pot to the platter. Let the pork rest for 10 minutes before slicing into six equal pieces.

MACRONUTRIENTS:

| Calories: 339 | Carbs: 5.5 g | Protein: 58.1 g |
| Fat: 9.1 g | Fiber: 4 g | Net Carbs: 1.5 g |

TAKE-OUT STYLE ORANGE CHICKEN

SERVES 6

PREP TIME: 5M

COOK TIME: 10M

TOTAL TIME: 15M

¼ cup (60 ml) soy sauce (or coconut aminos)

¼ cup (60 ml) + 3 tablespoons (45 ml) water, divided

¼ cup (48 g) powdered erythritol

½ teaspoon orange extract

½ teaspoon orange zest

½ teaspoon garlic powder

Pinch of crushed red pepper flakes (optional)

2 pounds (908 g) boneless, skinless chicken breasts, cut into 1" (2.5 cm) pieces

1½ tablespoons (9 g) arrowroot powder

Orange chicken is a beloved take-out meal in our house. This recipe is sugar free but still embodies all the flavors of a citrusy, sweet, and tangy orange chicken. I love to serve this over a big bed of fried cauliflower rice and steamed broccoli—and of course, don't forget the chopsticks.

In a small bowl, whisk together the soy sauce, ¼ cup (60 ml) of the water, powdered erythritol, orange extract, orange zest, and garlic powder. If you like a spicier orange chicken, add the crushed red pepper flakes.

Add the chicken to the pot and pour the marinade over the top.

Close the lid and seal the vent. Cook on HIGH pressure for 7 minutes. Quick release the steam. Press CANCEL.

Use a slotted spoon to remove the chicken from the pot and place in a large bowl. Strain the marinade to catch any loose bits from the chicken. Return the marinade to the pot and press the SAUTÉ button.

In a small bowl or measuring cup, whisk together the remaining 3 tablespoons (45 ml) water and the arrowroot powder to form a slurry. When the marinade begins to boil, whisk in the slurry. Continue whisking as the mixture thickens and becomes sticky, 2 to 3 minutes.

Pour the sauce on top of the chicken and toss to coat.

MACRONUTRIENTS:

Calories: 188	Carbs: 2.6 g	Protein: 35.7 g
Fat: 4 g	Fiber: 0.1 g	Net Carbs: 2.5 g

SHRIMP ÉTOUFFÉE

SERVES 8

PREP TIME: 10M

COOK TIME: 12M

TOTAL TIME: 22M

3½ ounces (100 g) diced green bell pepper

3 ounces (84 g) diced carrot

1½ ounces (42 g) diced onion

1 rib celery, diced

2 tablespoons (28 g) butter

1 can (14 ounces, or 392 g) diced tomatoes

10 ounces (280 g) frozen okra

1 can (7 ounces, or 196 g) diced green chiles

½ cup (120 ml) chicken broth

1½ teaspoons crab boil seasoning

½ teaspoon salt

1 pound (454 g) large shrimp, peeled and deveined

Étouffée is a Cajun stew that's thick and spicy. Traditional étouffée is made by combining butter and flour to make a roux, and the whole thing is served over a big bed of rice. To make it keto friendly, I omitted the roux and the rice—but not the flavor. If you like spicy foods, dial up the heat by adding cayenne pepper before cooking. Keep it traditional by serving it with "rice," in this case Mexican Cauliflower Rice (page 20).

Turn the pot to SAUTÉ mode. Once hot, add the bell pepper, carrot, onion, celery, and butter. Sauté for 2 to 3 minutes to soften the vegetables. Press CANCEL.

Add the tomatoes, okra, green chiles, broth, crab boil seasoning, and salt.

Close the lid and seal the vent. Cook on HIGH pressure for 8 minutes. Quick release the steam.

Add the shrimp to the pot. Close the lid and seal the vent. Cook for an additional 2 minutes on HIGH pressure. Quick release the steam.

MACRONUTRIENTS:

Calories: 107	Carbs: 6.9 g	Protein: 13.1 g
Fat: 3.2 g	Fiber: 1.9 g	Net Carbs: 5 g

STICKY COUNTRY RIBS

SERVES 8

PREP TIME: 5M

COOK TIME: 40M

TOTAL TIME: 45M

4 pounds (1816 g) country-style pork ribs

¼ cup (60 ml) soy sauce (or coconut aminos)

¼ cup (60 ml) water

2 tablespoons (40 g) sugar-free strawberry jelly

2 tablespoons (32 g) brown sugar substitute

½ teaspoon xanthan gum

Believe it or not, I did not discover country ribs until recently. I don't know how I lived so many years without them because, my oh my, they're scrumptious! Despite their name, country-style ribs are boneless and very meaty. This recipe is excellent for both a weeknight supper or a Fourth of July cookout.

Place the ribs in the pot.

In a small bowl, whisk together the soy sauce, water, jelly, and brown sugar substitute.

Pour the marinade over the ribs.

Close the lid and seal the vent. Cook on HIGH pressure for 25 minutes. Quick release the steam. Press CANCEL.

Remove the ribs to a baking sheet and cover with aluminum foil. Heat the broiler.

Turn the pot to SAUTÉ mode. When a light boil begins, sprinkle in the xanthan gum and whisk continuously while the sauce thickens, 3 to 4 minutes. You should have about 1½ cups (360 ml) of sauce.

Brush the ribs with a thick layer of sauce. Broil for 5 minutes, remove from the oven, and brush again. Broil until the sauce is sticky and glazed on the ribs, another 5 minutes. Serve with extra sauce for dipping.

Note: Little pieces of meat may fall off during cooking and be in the juices. You may want to run the juices through a fine-mesh sieve before making the sauce.

Complete the Meal: Broccoli with Garlic-Herb Cheese Sauce (page 158) Twice-Baked Mashed Cauliflower (page 173) Maple Bacon Corn Bread (page 165)

MACRONUTRIENTS:

Calories: 485	Carbs: 2.6 g	Protein: 51 g
Fat: 30 g	Fiber: 1.6 g	Net Carbs: 1 g

TERIYAKI CHICKEN

SERVES 4

PREP TIME: 5M

COOK TIME: 13M

TOTAL TIME: 18M

½ cup (120 ml) soy sauce
(or coconut aminos)

¼ cup (60 ml) +
3 tablespoons (45 ml)
water, divided

2 scallions, sliced

2 tablespoons (32 g)
brown sugar substitute

1 tablespoon (15 ml) rice
vinegar

1 tablespoon (6 g) ginger
paste (or freshly grated
ginger)

1 teaspoon garlic powder
(or 3 cloves garlic,
minced)

1½ pounds (680 g)
boneless, skinless
chicken breasts, cut
into 1" (2.5 cm) pieces

1½ tablespoons (9 g)
arrowroot powder

Sesame seeds (optional)

In case you haven't noticed, I have a love affair with Asian food. The sweet and salty sauces give me all the feels. Teriyaki chicken has long been a favorite of mine at hibachi restaurants, and it's a snap to whip up at home. I like to serve it with sautéed zucchini, mushrooms, and fried cauliflower rice.

In a large measuring cup, whisk together the soy sauce, ¼ cup (60 ml) of the water, scallions, brown sugar substitute, rice vinegar, ginger, and garlic powder.

Pour the marinade into the pot and add the chicken.

Close the lid and seal the vent. Cook on HIGH pressure for 5 minutes. Quick release the steam. Press CANCEL.

Use a slotted spoon to remove the chicken from the pot. Pour the marinade through a fine-mesh sieve to remove any bits of chicken left behind. Return the marinade to the pot.

In a small cup, whisk together the remaining 3 tablespoons (45 ml) water and the arrowroot powder to form a slurry.

Turn the pot to SAUTÉ mode. Let the mixture come to a light boil and whisk in the slurry. Whisk continuously as the sauce thickens, 2 to 3 minutes.

Pour the sauce over the chicken. Top with the sesame seeds, if using.

MACRONUTRIENTS:

Calories: 217	Carbs: 6 g	Protein: 39.7 g
Fat: 3 g	Fiber: 0.4 g	Net Carbs: 5.6 g

PIZZA-STUFFED CHICKEN

SERVES: 4

PREP TIME: 10M

COOK TIME: 12M

TOTAL TIME: 22M

2 pounds (907 g) chicken breasts (about 4 pieces)

4 ounces (115 g) cream cheese, softened

½ teaspoon salt

1 teaspoon dried basil

½ teaspoon dried oregano

¾ teaspoon garlic powder

½ cup (70 g) green bell pepper, cut in strips

About 16 slices (20 g) pepperoni

½ cup (120 ml) water

4 slices provolone cheese

½ cup (120 ml) low-carb marinara sauce

ACCESSORY NEEDED:

Trivet

Who doesn't love pizza? My favorite combination of toppings is pepperoni and green pepper, which is the inspiration for this dish. You can customize your Pizza-Stuffed Chicken to include your favorite pizza toppings, but just be sure to adjust the macros! Pair your chicken with a crisp Caesar salad for a complete ultra-low-carb meal.

Place the chicken breasts on a cutting board. Pat dry with a paper towel. Butterfly the chicken open but do not cut all the way through.

In a small bowl, combine the cream cheese with the spices.

Stuff each breast with one-fourth each of the cream cheese mixture, bell pepper, and pepperoni. Use toothpicks to close the edges.

Pour the water into the pot. Place the trivet inside. Lay a piece of aluminum foil on top of the trivet and place the chicken breasts on top. It is okay if they overlap.

Heat the broiler.

Close the lid and seal the vent. Cook on HIGH pressure for 10 minutes. Quick release the steam.

Remove the toothpicks and place each breast on a baking sheet. Top each with one slice of provolone cheese. Broil 2 to 3 minutes, or until the cheese is melted and bubbly. Top each breast with one-fourth of the marinara sauce.

MACRONUTRIENTS:

Calories: 488	Carbs: 3.1 g	Protein: 60.2 g
Fat: 24.7 g	Fiber: 0.6 g	Net Carbs: 2.5 g

CHAPTER 9

Side Dishes

Forget the turkey—at Thanksgiving, I'm all about the side dishes! With the Instant Pot, there's no need to wait for November to roll around. In this chapter, several Southern classics get a keto make-over, including my favorite, Southern "Corn Bread" Dressing (page 166). It's a secret family recipe, though, so *shhh*, don't tell anyone! Side dishes and vegetables are also a great way to sneak in extra fat when needed. Using a steamer basket or small casserole dish in your Instant Pot will make your veggies taste like they've been slow cooking all day!

ROASTED GARLIC

YIELD: ¼ CUP (60 G)
    GARLIC PASTE
SERVES 4 (1 TABLESPOON,
    OR 15 G, EACH)
PREP TIME: 2M
COOK TIME: 25M
TOTAL TIME: 27M

4 bulbs garlic

**1 tablespoon (15 ml)
    avocado oil**

1 teaspoon salt

Pinch of black pepper

1 cup (240 ml) water

ACCESSORY NEEDED:

Steamer basket

Roasted garlic used to be one of those things that I loved but never made. Sure, making it in the oven is possible at home, but who has time for that when you're chasing kids, chauffeuring to sports, or any of the other million activities you have going on? Instead, you can use your Instant Pot to make roasted garlic in half the time, so you can keep it in your fridge to spice up all your favorite dishes!

Slice the pointy tops off the bulbs of garlic to expose the cloves.

Drizzle the avocado oil on top of the garlic and sprinkle with the salt and pepper.

Place the bulbs in the steamer basket, cut-side up. Alternatively, you may place them on a piece of aluminum foil with the sides pulled up and resting on top of the trivet. Place the steamer basket in the pot.

Close the lid and seal the vent. Cook on HIGH pressure for 25 minutes. Quick release the steam.

Let the garlic cool completely before removing the bulbs from the pot.

Hold the stem end (bottom) of the bulb and squeeze out all the garlic. Mash the cloves with a fork to make a paste.

Note: You can use this roasted garlic in sauces, burgers, vegetables, or soups to add a stronger garlic flavor.

MACRONUTRIENTS

Calories: 44	Carbs: 0.8 g	Protein: 0.2 g
Fat: 4.4 g	Fiber: 0 g	Net Carbs: 0.8 g

BACON JELLY

YIELD: 1½ CUPS (480 G)

SERVES 12

   (2 TABLESPOONS,

   OR 40 G, EACH)

PREP TIME: 10M

COOK TIME: 15M

TOTAL TIME: 25M

12 ounces (340 g) bacon, diced (about ½", or 13 mm)

8 ounces (227 g) onion, diced (about 1 large onion)

⅓ cup (80 ml) sugar-free maple syrup

¼ cup (64 g) brown sugar substitute

2 tablespoons (30 ml) apple cider vinegar

2 tablespoons (30 ml) water

1 teaspoon xanthan gum

My bacon cup runneth over. I'll be honest—one of the things that drew me to keto was that bacon was on the imaginary "approved" list. This Bacon Jelly is the condiment of all condiments. It may *look* a little funny when it's finished, but it tastes like heaven. Slather it on a piece of corn bread, a burger, or a slice of low-carb toast. Shoot, eat it with a spoon. This is a judgment-free zone!

Turn the pot to SAUTÉ mode. Once hot, add the bacon. Sauté until the bacon is just barely chewy and the fat is beginning to render, 2 to 3 minutes. Do not drain the grease.

Add the onion, syrup, brown sugar substitute, vinegar, and water. Give it a good stir to combine.

Close the lid and seal the vent. Cook on HIGH pressure for 10 minutes. Quick release the steam. Press CANCEL.

Turn the pot to SAUTÉ mode again. Let the mixture boil for 2 to 3 minutes so some of the liquid cooks down. Add the xanthan gum and whisk for another 1 to 2 minutes while the sauce thickens into a jelly.

Immediately transfer the jelly to a jar. Once cool, store in the refrigerator for up to 1 week.

Note: Use an immersion blender or food processor to make a smoother jelly, if desired. If your jelly becomes too thick during the final sauté, add a little water and whisk while it cooks.

Complete the Meal: Bacon and Cheddar–Stuffed Burgers (page 96)
Maple Bacon Corn Bread (page 165)

MACRONUTRIENTS:

Calories: 68	Carbs: 8.7 g	Protein: 3.5 g
Fat: 3.4 g	Fiber: 6.4 g	Net Carbs: 2.3 g

CREAMED SPINACH

SERVES 5

PREP TIME: 5M

COOK TIME: 16M

TOTAL TIME: 21M

1 teaspoon avocado oil

2 ounces (56 g) onion, diced

2 cloves garlic, minced

12 ounces (340 g) fresh spinach

½ cup (50 g) grated Parmesan cheese

3 ounces (84 g) cream cheese, softened

2 tablespoons (30 ml) heavy cream

1 teaspoon salt

½ cup (120 ml) water

ACCESSORIES NEEDED:

7" (18 cm) baking dish

Trivet

Everyone knows spinach is a superfood, but it's a *super* superfood for a ketogenic diet! Spinach is high in magnesium and potassium, electrolytes that are extremely important when you follow a ketogenic diet because your body does not retain as much water as it is used to. The lack of water can lead to keto flu, something no one wants to experience! This recipe for Creamed Spinach is a delectable way to add electrolytes to your diet.

Turn the pot to SAUTÉ mode. Once hot, add the avocado oil, onion, and garlic. Sauté until translucent, 2 to 3 minutes, and then add the spinach.

Cook until the spinach is wilted and the water is cooked out, about 5 minutes. Place the spinach on top of a paper towel and squeeze any excess water out.

Return the spinach to the pot and add the Parmesan, cream cheese, cream, and salt. Stir until the cheese is melted, 2 to 3 minutes.

Transfer the spinach mixture to the baking dish and cover with aluminum foil. Rinse out the inner pot and place back in the base. Add the water to the pot and place the trivet inside. Place the baking dish on the trivet.

Close the lid and seal the vent. Cook on HIGH pressure for 5 minutes. Quick release the steam.

Complete the Meal: Cod Fillets with Basil Butter (page 124)
Pork Tenderloin Medallions with Pan Sauce (page 140)
Beef Tenderloin with Red Wine Reduction (page 99)

MACRONUTRIENTS:

Calories: 145
Fat: 11 g

Carbs: 4.9 g
Fiber: 1.7 g

Protein: 6.5 g
Net Carbs: 3.2 g

BROCCOLI WITH GARLIC-HERB CHEESE SAUCE

SERVES 4

PREP TIME: 5M

COOK TIME: 3M

TOTAL TIME: 8M

½ cup (120 ml) water

1 pound (454 g) broccoli (frozen or fresh)

½ cup (120 ml) heavy cream

1 tablespoon (14 g) butter

½ cup (57 g) shredded Cheddar cheese

3 tablespoons (45 g) garlic and herb cheese spread (such as Boursin)

Pinch of salt

Pinch of black pepper

ACCESSORIES NEEDED:

Trivet

Steamer basket

Broccoli with cheese sauce is a timeless combination that both adults and kids enjoy. For some of you, it might be the only way you can get your kids to eat broccoli! I jazzed up the old standard by adding garlic and herb cheese spread to the sauce. You can find these soft creamy cheeses in any grocery store, typically in the deli area. So go on and enjoy this grown-up version of broccoli and cheese!

Add the water to the pot and place the trivet inside.

Put the steamer basket on top of the trivet. Place the broccoli in the basket.

Close the lid and seal the vent. Cook on LOW pressure for 1 minute. Quick release the steam. Press CANCEL.

Carefully remove the steamer basket from the pot and drain the water. If you steamed a full bunch of broccoli, pull the florets off the stem. (Chop the stem into bite-size pieces—it's surprisingly creamy.)

Turn the pot to SAUTÉ mode. Add the cream and butter. Stir continuously while the butter melts and the cream warms up.

When the cream begins to bubble on the edges, add the Cheddar cheese, cheese spread, salt, and pepper. Whisk continuously until the cheeses are melted and a sauce consistency is reached, 1 to 2 minutes.

Top one-fourth of the broccoli with 2 tablespoons (30 ml) cheese sauce per serving.

Note: The sauce recipe yields 1 cup (240 ml). Use the leftover sauce to mix with Shredded Chicken (page 114) or add to scrambled eggs for a fancier breakfast! Leftover sauce may be refrigerated for up to 1 week.

Complete the Meal: Crispy Chicken Thighs with Gravy (page 129) Sticky Country Ribs (page 149)

MACRONUTRIENTS:

Calories: 134	Carbs: 4.6 g	Protein: 4 g
Fat: 11.6 g	Fiber: 1.5 g	Net Carbs: 3.1 g

EASY MARINARA SAUCE

YIELD: 7 CUPS (1715 G)

SERVES 28 (¼ CUP, OR
61 G, EACH)

PREP TIME: 5M

COOK TIME: 15M

TOTAL TIME: 20M

1 cup (240 ml) water

2 cans (28 ounces, or
784 g, each) crushed
tomatoes

2 tablespoons (30 g)
tomato paste

2 tablespoons (24 g)
granulated erythritol

2 tablespoons (6 g)
dried basil

1 tablespoon (15 g)
Roasted Garlic (page
155) or 4 cloves garlic,
minced

1½ teaspoons Italian
seasoning

1 teaspoon onion powder

½ teaspoon salt

A basic marinara sauce is one of the best recipes you can have in your keto repertoire. Use it in keto-friendly homemade pizzas and pastas or as a dip for your favorite frying cheese. Many jarred marinara sauces contain preservatives and sugar, which make them unsuitable for a ketogenic diet. This recipe is easy and cooks quickly in your Instant Pot. You can freeze the sauce in 1-quart (1 L) resealable plastic bags so that you always have some on hand.

Add the water to the pot.

In a bowl, combine the crushed tomatoes, tomato paste, erythritol, basil, Roasted Garlic, Italian seasoning, onion powder, and salt.

Add the tomato mixture to the pot but do not stir.

Close the lid and seal the vent. Cook on HIGH pressure for 15 minutes. Quick release the steam.

Note: A little bit of burned sauce might be on the bottom of your pot. This is normal due to the acidity of the tomatoes.

MACRONUTRIENTS:

| Calories: 28 | Carbs: 4.9 g | Protein: 1.1 g |
| Fat: 0 g | Fiber: 1.6 g | Net Carbs: 3.3 g |

FAUX MAC AND CHEESE

SERVES 6

PREP TIME: 5M

COOK TIME: 5M

TOTAL TIME: 10M

1 large head cauliflower
(about 2 pounds, or
908 g)

½ cup (120 ml) water

½ cup (120 ml) heavy
cream

2 ounces (56 g) cream
cheese, softened

1 teaspoon Dijon mustard

¼ teaspoon
Worcestershire sauce

¼ teaspoon salt

Pinch of black pepper

2 cups (230 g) shredded
Cheddar cheese

ACCESSORIES NEEDED:

Steamer basket

7" (18 cm) baking dish

Where I come from, mac and cheese is a vegetable served alongside fried chicken. My adoration for the dish will never wither, but the longer I live a ketogenic lifestyle, the more I embrace keto-friendly substitutes for those beloved comfort foods. In this faux version of mac and cheese, steamed cauliflower takes the place of noodles and is coated in a silky-smooth cheese sauce.

Place the cauliflower on a cutting board. Remove the core and leaves but do not completely de-core. The head should remain intact for cooking.

Place the cauliflower in the steamer basket and lower into the Instant Pot. Add the water to the pot.

Close the lid and seal the vent. Cook on LOW pressure for 3 minutes. Quick release the steam. Press CANCEL.

Remove the lid and use a fork to check for doneness. The fork should easily penetrate the cauliflower, but it should not fall apart. If it is still very firm, cook for 1 additional minute on LOW pressure.

Place the cauliflower back on the cutting board and remove the florets from the stems. Place the florets in the baking dish and set aside.

Drain the water from the pot. Turn the pot to SAUTÉ mode. Add the cream to the pot.

Add the cream cheese, mustard, Worcestershire, salt, and pepper. Whisk until the cream cheese is completely melted, 1 to 2 minutes.

Add the Cheddar and whisk until all the cheese is melted and the consistency is smooth, 1 to 2 minutes.

Pour the cheese sauce over the cauliflower and toss to coat.

Optional: If desired, place under the broiler for 1 minute to crisp up the top. Let the dish rest for a few minutes before serving so the sauce has time to thicken.

MACRONUTRIENTS:

| Calories: 387 | Carbs: 8.2 g | Protein: 21.4 g |
| Fat: 31 g | Fiber: 2 g | Net Carbs: 6.2 g |

HORSERADISH WHIPPED CAULIFLOWER

SERVES 5

PREP TIME: 5M

COOK TIME: 5M

TOTAL TIME: 10M

½ cup (120 ml) water

1 head cauliflower
(1½ pounds, or
680 g), stem and
leaves removed

2 tablespoons (30 g)
sour cream

1½ teaspoons horseradish
(or more, if desired)

½ teaspoon garlic powder

½ teaspoon salt

¼ teaspoon black pepper

1 to 2 tablespoons (15 to
30 ml) heavy cream
(optional)

ACCESSORY NEEDED:

Steamer basket

One of my favorite local steakhouses in town used to serve a savory horseradish mashed potato that was just to die for. I loved it so much, it inspired me to make a low-carb version using cauliflower in place of potatoes. I like to use fresh cauliflower for my cauli-mash because it becomes softer and less mealy than frozen cauliflower. A quality food processor will also help you achieve that silky-smooth texture that is reminiscent of mashed potatoes.

Add the water to the Instant Pot. Place the steamer basket inside and add the cauliflower.

Close the lid and seal the vent. Cook on LOW pressure for 5 minutes. Quick release the steam.

Remove the lid and check for doneness. The cauliflower should fall apart at the touch and be very soft. If it is still firm, cook for an additional 1 to 2 minutes on LOW pressure.

Remove the steamer basket from the pot and transfer the cauliflower to the bowl of a food processor.

Pulse in the food processor a few times to break up the florets. Add the sour cream, horseradish, garlic powder, salt, and pepper, and blend until smooth and creamy. If needed, add the cream to thin out the mash, but you will need to recalculate the macros.

Complete the Meal: French Dip Roast Beef (page 101)
Pork Chops with Maple-Dijon Cream Sauce (page 138)

MACRONUTRIENTS:

| Calories: 51 | Carbs: 8 g | Protein: 3.1 g |
| Fat: 1.6 g | Fiber: 3.1 g | Net Carbs: 5.1 g |

ROSEMARY MUSHROOMS

SERVES 2

PREP TIME: 5M

COOK TIME: 15M

TOTAL TIME: 20M

8 ounces (227 g) sliced mushrooms

¼ cup (60 ml) dry red wine (such as Cabernet Sauvignon)

2 tablespoons (30 ml) beef broth

½ teaspoon garlic powder

¼ teaspoon Worcestershire sauce

Pinch of salt

Pinch of black pepper

¼ teaspoon xanthan gum

Mushrooms are one of my favorite side dishes because not only do they take on any flavors in your meal, but they are also a powerhouse of nutrients. Mushrooms are low in calories and full of B vitamins and potassium. Potassium is one of the three major electrolytes and a critical component of a ketogenic diet. These flavorful mushrooms are an excellent accompaniment to just about any meal in this book—or elsewhere!

Add the mushrooms, wine, broth, garlic powder, Worcestershire sauce, salt, and pepper to the pot.

Close the lid and seal the vent. Cook on HIGH pressure for 13 minutes. Quick release the steam. Press CANCEL.

Turn the pot to SAUTÉ mode. Add the xanthan gum and whisk until the juices have thickened, 1 to 2 minutes.

Complete the Meal: Beef Tenderloin with Red Wine Reduction (page 99) Pork Tenderloin Medallions with Pan Sauce (page 140)

MACRONUTRIENTS:

Calories: 94

Fat: 0.4 g

Carbs: 7.9 g

Fiber: 2.9 g

Protein: 3.8 g

Net Carbs: 5 g

MAPLE BACON CORN BREAD

SERVES 8

PREP TIME: 5M

COOK TIME: 30M

TOTAL TIME: 35M

1¼ cups (140 g) almond flour

1 teaspoon baking powder

1 teaspoon granulated erythritol

⅓ teaspoon salt

4 tablespoons (56 g) butter, softened, plus more for greasing the dish

3 eggs

2 tablespoons (30 ml) sugar-free maple syrup

¼ cup (20 g) bacon bits

½ cup (120 ml) water

ACCESSORIES NEEDED:

7" (18 cm) baking dish

Trivet

If I had to name one of the most iconic Southern foods, corn bread would be high on the list. What's a bowl of chili without corn bread, anyway? Even though there are zero grains in this recipe, the textures and flavors mimic traditional corn bread to a tee. You'll want to make a double batch of these, trust me!

In a medium bowl, combine the almond flour, baking powder, erythritol, and salt. Add the butter and use a fork to work it into the dry mix. A dough similar to cookie dough should form.

Add the eggs and maple syrup and mix with a fork until combined. There will be lumps in the batter. Fold in the bacon bits.

Grease the baking dish with butter or line it with parchment paper. Pour the batter into the dish and cover tightly with aluminum foil.

Add the water to pot. Place the dish on the trivet and lower it into the pot.

Close the lid and seal the vent. Cook on HIGH pressure for 30 minutes. Quick release the steam.

Remove the dish from the pot and remove the foil. Let the corn bread rest for 10 minutes before flipping out onto a plate.

Note: Mix in a little brown sugar substitute and cinnamon to softened butter for a sweet spread for your corn bread.

Complete the Meal: First Place Chili (page 69)
Cauliflower and Bacon Chowder (page 63)
Un-Sloppy Joes (page 107)

MACRONUTRIENTS:

Calories: 220	Carbs: 4 g	Protein: 8 g
Fat: 18 g	Fiber: 2 g	Net Carbs: 2 g

SOUTHERN "CORN BREAD" DRESSING

SERVES 6

PREP TIME: 5M

COOK TIME: 40M

TOTAL TIME: 45M

2½ cups (280 g) almond flour

2 tablespoons (4 g) ground sage

2 teaspoons baking powder

½ teaspoon salt

3 eggs

4 tablespoons (56 g) butter, melted

3 ounces (84 g) finely diced onion

2 ounces (56 g) finely diced celery (about 2 ribs)

1 cup (240 ml) chicken broth

Cooking spray

½ cup (120 ml) water

ACCESSORIES NEEDED:

7" (18 cm) baking dish

Trivet

Y'all, this is my favorite dish in this entire cookbook! If I've said that already, I take it back because this dressing is the bee's knees. Corn bread dressing is not to be confused with stuffing. Oh no, darlin', they're two completely different dishes. This corn bread dressing is exactly like the one my Gran makes everything Thanksgiving, but it's low carb and gluten free. All we're missing with this one is a big front porch and a glass of sweet tea!

In a large bowl, whisk together the almond flour, sage, baking powder, and salt. Whisk well to remove any lumps.

Add the eggs and butter and whisk together until well combined. Fold in the onion and celery.

Slowly add the broth and whisk until well combined. The mixture will be very thin and runny.

Spray the baking dish with cooking spray and transfer the corn bread mixture to the dish.

Add the water to the pot. Place the baking dish on the trivet and carefully lower it into the pot.

Close the lid and seal the vent. Cook on HIGH pressure for 40 minutes. Quick release the steam.

Note: Add leftover chicken or turkey to the uncooked corn bread mixture for a chicken/turkey-and-dressing casserole.

Complete the Meal: Anytime Thanksgiving Turkey (page 116)
Salisbury Steak (page 109)
Roast Chicken (page 115)

MACRONUTRIENTS:

Calories: 415	Carbs: 10.9 g	Protein: 13.6 g
Fat: 35 g	Fiber: 5.7 g	Net Carbs: 5.2 g

SOUTHERN-STYLE GREEN BEANS

SERVES 8

PREP TIME: 5M

COOK TIME: 30M

TOTAL TIME: 35M

3 bags (12 ounces, or 340 g, each) frozen cut green beans

1½ cups (360 ml) water

4 slices bacon, cut into 1" (2.5 cm) pieces

2 tablespoons (30 ml) bacon grease

2 teaspoons onion powder

2 teaspoons garlic powder

1½ teaspoons salt

1 teaspoon black pepper

Slow-cooked green beans are one of my favorite vegetables. Green beans are slightly higher in carbohydrates, but if you plan your day accordingly, they can easily fit into your macros. Despite their name, green beans are not part of the legume family, so they are an acceptable addition to your keto diet. These green beans take minimal effort and will taste like they've been cooking all day.

Add the green beans, water, bacon, bacon grease, onion powder, garlic powder, salt, and pepper to the pot. Stir to coat the beans evenly.

Close the lid and seal the vent. Cook on HIGH pressure for 30 minutes. Quick release the steam.

Note: Ramp up the flavor by adding a ham bone to the beans before cooking.

Complete the Meal: Holiday Spiral Ham (page 131) Kentucky Hot Brown Casserole (page 83)

MACRONUTRIENTS:

| Calories: 100 | Carbs: 8.8 g | Protein: 3.3 g |
| Fat: 4.7 g | Fiber: 3.3 g | Net Carbs: 5.5 g |

SPAGHETTI SQUASH ALFREDO

SERVES 6

PREP TIME: 5M

COOK TIME: 13M

TOTAL TIME: 18M

**1 spaghetti squash
(3 pounds, or 1362 g)**

1 cup (240 ml) water

**1 cup (240 ml) jarred
Alfredo sauce (about
half a 15-ounce, or
420 g, jar)**

**1 cup (150 g) frozen
green peas**

**4 ounces (112 g) diced
pancetta or bacon,
cooked**

**¼ cup (25 g) grated
Parmesan cheese**

ACCESSORY NEEDED:

Trivet

Spaghetti squash is a great substitute for pasta on a ketogenic diet. When cooked, the squash becomes stringy like spaghetti and grabs onto sauces. It's full of fiber and low in carbohydrates too. Spaghetti squash can typically take upwards of an hour to roast in the oven, but your Instant Pot gets the job done in less than 10 minutes!

Before cooking, make sure your spaghetti squash will fit in your instant pot. If it is too long, cut off the ends of the squash.

Cut the squash in half lengthwise. Use a spoon to scoop out the stringy parts and seeds.

Place the trivet in the pot and set the squash on top of the trivet. Lay them down however they will fit.

Add the water to the pot. Close the lid and seal the vent. Cook on HIGH pressure for 8 minutes. Quick release the steam. Press CANCEL.

Carefully remove the squash from the pot. Use a fork to check for doneness. The spaghetti strands should easily pull apart from the squash. If they do not, place it back in the pot and cook for 1 to 2 minutes on HIGH. Pull all the strands out of the squash.

Remove the trivet and drain the water from the pot.

Turn the pot to SAUTÉ mode. Add the spaghetti squash strands, Alfredo sauce, peas, and pancetta or bacon to the pot. Cook until heated through, 3 to 4 minutes, stirring to prevent burning.

Transfer the "pasta" to a bowl. Add the cheese and stir to combine.

Note: Macros are not calculated for the squash because each squash will yield a different amount of "spaghetti." Weigh your cooked spaghetti squash strands and calculate the macros using a fitness app.

Complete the Meal: Roast Chicken (page 115)

MACRONUTRIENTS FOR THE SAUCE:

Calories: 151	Carbs: 4.4 g	Protein: 7.5 g
Fat: 11.6 g	Fiber: 1 g	Net Carbs: 3.3 g

SWEET COUNTRY CARROTS

SERVES 4

PREP TIME: 5M

COOK TIME: 12M

TOTAL TIME: 27M

1 pound (454 g) baby
carrots

½ cup (120 ml) water

¼ cup (64 g) brown sugar
substitute

¼ cup (60 ml) sugar-free
maple syrup

4 tablespoons (56 g)
butter

½ teaspoon allspice

Pinch of salt

½ teaspoon xanthan gum
(optional)

These carrots remind me of the honey-glazed kind you can find at just about any country diner. The Instant Pot makes them perfectly tender in just a few minutes. While carrots do have a higher carb count than some vegetables, they're perfectly fine to eat if they're within your macros. Besides, I don't think anyone ever gained weight by eating too many carrots! You will definitely want to save this recipe for your Thanksgiving menu.

Combine the carrots, water, brown sugar substitute, maple syrup, butter, allspice, and salt in the pot. Stir to combine.

Close the lid and seal the vent. Cook on HIGH pressure for 12 minutes. Quick release the steam.

Remove the lid. Let the carrots rest for 10 minutes before serving so the glaze adheres to them.

Optional: Use a slotted spoon to remove the carrots to a bowl and thicken the sauce on SAUTÉ mode with the xanthan gum, if desired. This is not calculated in the macros.

Complete the Meal: Anytime Thanksgiving Turkey (page 116)
Sauerkraut Pork Roast (page 144)

MACRONUTRIENTS:

Calories: 172	Carbs: 24.5 g	Protein: 0.7 g
Fat: 11.2 g	Fiber: 17.3 g	Net Carbs: 7.2 g

SWEET ONION RELISH

YIELD: 2 CUPS (490 G)

SERVES 16

  (2 TABLESPOONS, OR

  30 G, EACH)

PREP TIME: 10M

COOK TIME: 33M

TOTAL TIME: 43M

1 pound (454 g) sweet
  Vidalia onions

2 tablespoons (28 g)
  butter

3 tablespoons (45 ml)
  water

¼ teaspoon baking soda

¼ teaspoon xanthan gum
  (optional)

If you haven't noticed yet, I am all about sauces, gravies, and spreads. I love to dip, dunk, and slather my food! This relish recipe came about by accident, and I am totally okay with that. If you've ever eaten creamed corn, this relish is quite similar. Sweet Vidalia onions cook down into a relish that is wonderful on top of roasts, burgers, or, if you're like me, right off the spoon!

Slice the ends off the onions. Peel the outer layer and discard. Slice the onions into thick rings, then cut the rings into large pieces.

Turn the pot to SAUTÉ mode and add the butter. Once melted, add the onions and cook for 5 minutes, stirring occasionally. Press CANCEL.

Add the water to pot. Close the lid and seal the vent. Cook on HIGH pressure for 20 minutes. Quick release the steam. Press CANCEL.

Turn the pot to SAUTÉ mode and let the onion mixture come to a low bubble. Add the baking soda and stir. The mixture will bubble up and begin to cook down. Sauté until the liquid has evaporated and a thick sauce has formed, 8 to 10 minutes.

Transfer to a jar. Once cool, store in the refrigerator for up to 1 week.

Optional: Add the xanthan gum during the second sauté for a more jelly-like texture, if desired. This is not calculated in the macros.

Complete the Meal: Maple Bacon Corn Bread (page 165)
Bacon and Cheddar–Stuffed Burgers (page 96)
Anytime Thanksgiving Turkey (page 116)

MACRONUTRIENTS:

Calories: 24	Carbs: 2.6 g	Protein: 0.3 g
Fat: 1.4 g	Fiber: 0.6 g	Net Carbs: 2.0 g

TWICE-BAKED MASHED CAULIFLOWER

SERVES 4

PREP TIME: 10M

COOK TIME: 5M

TOTAL TIME: 15M

½ cup (120 ml) water

1 head cauliflower (about 2 pounds, or 908 g)

2 ounces (56 g) cream cheese

½ teaspoon salt

¼ teaspoon garlic powder

¼ cup (30 g) shredded Cheddar cheese

¼ cup (20 g) bacon bits

ACCESSORIES NEEDED:

Steamer basket

7" (18 cm) baking dish

Trivet

If there were an award for most versatile vegetable, cauliflower would take first place. Cauliflower can be transformed to take on virtually any form, whether it be mashed potatoes, fried rice, or pizza crust. Bonus: It's full of vitamins and minerals, high in fiber, and low in calories. In this recipe, steamed cauliflower replicates twice-baked mashed potatoes for a cheesy and creamy low-carb side dish!

Pour the water into the pot. Add the steamer basket.

Cut the cauliflower into quarters. Cut out the stems on each quarter. Cut the quarters into small florets and place them in the steamer basket.

Close the lid and seal the vent. Cook on STEAM mode for 2 minutes. Quick release the steam.

Transfer the cauliflower to a food processor. Add the cream cheese, salt, and garlic powder. Pulse until smooth.

Transfer the cauliflower mixture to the baking dish. Fold in the Cheddar cheese and bacon bits.

Cover the dish tightly with aluminum foil. Place it on the trivet and carefully lower it into the pot. Cook on LOW pressure for 3 minutes. Quick release the steam.

Note: If you don't have a food processor, you can use a small blender or an immersion blender. If your Instant Pot does not have the STEAM setting, use HIGH pressure for the same amount of time.

Complete the Meal: Baby Back Ribs with BBQ Glaze (page 95)
Bacon and Cheddar–Stuffed Burgers (page 96)

MACRONUTRIENTS:

| Calories: 130 | Carbs: 8.4 g | Protein 6.7 g |
| Fat: 7.8 g | Fiber: 3.6 g | Net Carbs: 4.8 g |

CHAPTER 10

Desserts

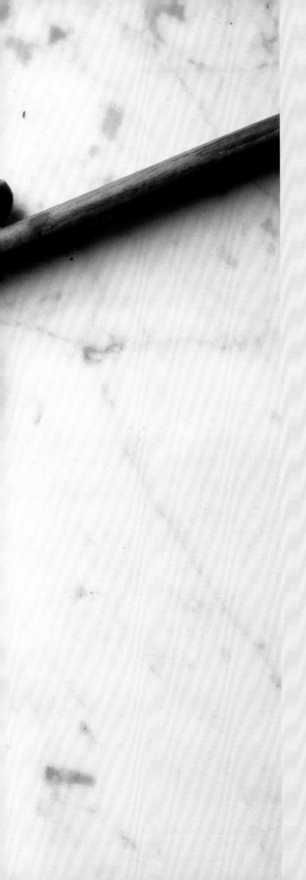

essert. Must I really say more? I was born with a major affinity for the sweeter things in life, specifically crème brûlée. When I first received my Instant Pot, I was amazed that I could use it to make dessert! Following a ketogenic diet hasn't stopped me from enjoying a keto-friendly sweet treat on occasion . . . okay . . . on the regular. The recipes in this chapter will make you feel indulgent without blowing your macros out of the water. So go ahead, have the extra bite!

CANDIED PECANS

SERVES 8

PREP TIME: 5M

COOK TIME: 18M

TOTAL TIME: 23M

4 cups (440 g) raw pecan halves

¼ cup (60 ml) sugar-free maple syrup

2 tablespoons (32 g) brown sugar substitute

2 tablespoons (28 g) butter

2 teaspoons ground cinnamon

1 tablespoon (15 ml) water

Have you ever walked through a mall and smelled candied nuts wafting through the air? That sugary sweet smell is intoxicating! Homemade candied pecans are so easy to make, and they also make a great gift for new neighbors, teachers, or friends. Your Instant Pot cooks these nuts in a fraction of the time it would traditionally take. You can eat them straight from the jar or add them to your favorite cakes and pies!

Heat the oven to 350°F (180°C, or gas mark 4). Line a baking sheet with parchment paper.

Add the pecans, syrup, brown sugar substitute, butter, cinnamon, and water to the pot and stir to coat.

Turn the pot to SAUTÉ mode and cook for 5 minutes, stirring continuously. Press CANCEL.

Close the lid and seal the vent. Cook on HIGH pressure for 10 minutes. Quick release the steam.

Transfer the pecans and all the syrup to the prepared baking sheet. Spread them in a single layer.

Bake until the sauce begins to caramelize and the pecans get sticky, 3 to 5 minutes. Watch closely so the nuts do not burn. Cool completely before storing in an airtight container.

MACRONUTRIENTS:

Calories: 150	Carbs: 3.6 g	Protein: 1.7 g
Fat: 13.7 g	Fiber: 1.4 g	Net Carbs: 2.2 g

CHOCOLATE CAKE WITH WHIPPED CHOCOLATE FROSTING

SERVES 8

PREP TIME: 10M

COOK TIME: 35M

TOTAL TIME: 45M +
  COOLING TIME

This wouldn't be a proper cookbook without a recipe for chocolate cake. Gluten-free and sugar-free baking needn't be bland and boring. This chocolate cake is as decadent as they come. Serve it with an ice-cold glass of almond milk and satisfy all your chocolate cravings!

FOR CAKE:

2 cups (224 g) almond
  flour

1 cup (200 g) granulated
  erythritol

⅓ cup (40 g) unsweetened
  cocoa powder

1½ teaspoons baking
  powder

Pinch of salt

4 eggs

1 teaspoon vanilla extract

½ cup (112 g) butter,
  melted and cooled

6 tablespoons (90 ml)
  strong coffee, cooled

Cooking spray

½ cup (120 ml) water

To make the cake: In a large bowl, whisk together the almond flour, granulated erythritol, cocoa powder, baking powder, and salt. Whisk well to remove any lumps.

Add the eggs and vanilla and mix with a hand mixer on low speed until combined.

With the mixer still on low speed, slowly add the melted butter and mix until well combined.

Add the coffee and mix on low speed until the batter is thoroughly combined. Scrape the sides and bottom of the bowl to make sure everything is well mixed.

Spray the cake pan with cooking spray. Pour the batter into the pan. Cover tightly with aluminum foil.

Add the water to the pot. Place the cake pan on the trivet and carefully lower it into the pot.

Close the lid and seal the vent. Cook on HIGH pressure for 35 minutes. Quick release the steam.

Carefully remove the cake pan from the pot and place on a wire rack to cool. Flip the cake onto a plate once it is cool enough to touch. Cool completely before frosting.

½ cup (112 g) butter, softened

4 ounces (112 g) cream cheese, softened

¼ teaspoon vanilla extract

2½ tablespoons (30 g) powdered erythritol

2 tablespoons (16 g) unsweetened cocoa powder

ACCESSORIES NEEDED:

7" (18 cm) Bundt pan or cake pan

Trivet

To make the frosting: In a medium bowl, use the mixer to whip the butter, cream cheese, and vanilla until light and fluffy, 1 to 2 minutes. With the mixer running, slowly add the powdered erythritol and cocoa powder. Mix until everything is well combined.

Once the cake is completely cooled, spread the frosting on the top and down the sides.

MACRONUTRIENTS:

Calories: 476	Carbs: 8.7 g	Protein: 10.9 g
Fat: 44.3 g	Fiber: 4.4 g	Net Carbs: 4.3 g

CRÈME BRÛLÉE

SERVES 4

PREP TIME: 5M

COOK TIME: 30M

TOTAL TIME: 35M + 2H
    CHILL TIME

5 egg yolks (whites reserved for another use)

5 tablespoons (60 g) powdered erythritol

1½ cups (360 ml) heavy cream

2 teaspoons vanilla extract

2 cups (480 ml) water

1 teaspoon tagatose, divided (optional, see Note)

ACCESSORIES NEEDED:

Trivet

Four (4-ounce, or 112 g) ramekins

Forget all the times I said I had a favorite recipe in this cookbook because THIS is my favorite recipe. Before keto, on the rare occasions my husband and I were able to go to an adult restaurant, I would always check the dessert menu first to see whether they had crème brûlée. It was never a dessert I made at home because it seemed too complicated. Let me assure you, it's truly so simple! The Instant Pot does all the hard work, so you can just enjoy a homemade version of this restaurant classic.

In a small bowl, use a fork to break up the egg yolks. Stir in the erythritol.

Pour the cream into a small saucepan over medium-low heat and let it warm up, 3 to 4 minutes. Do not let it boil. Remove the saucepan from the heat.

Temper the egg yolks by slowly adding a small spoonful of the warm cream, whisking the entire time. Do this three times to make sure the egg yolks are fully tempered (slightly warmed up). You do not want scrambled eggs in your crème brûlée!

Slowly add the tempered eggs to the cream, whisking the whole time. Add the vanilla and whisk again.

Pour the cream mixture into the ramekins. Each ramekin should have ½ cup (120 ml) liquid. Cover each with aluminum foil.

Place the trivet inside the Instant Pot. Add the water. Carefully place the ramekins on top of the trivet. You may stack them up in a pyramid shape if they do not all fit.

Close the lid and seal the vent. Cook on HIGH pressure for 11 minutes. Let the steam naturally release for 15 minutes before manually releasing.

Carefully remove a ramekin from the pot. Remove the foil and check for doneness. The custard should be mostly set with a slightly jiggly center. Place all the ramekins in the fridge for 2 hours to chill and set.

Optional: If desired, sprinkle ¼ teaspoon tagatose on top of each ramekin and use a kitchen torch to caramelize it. This will give the crème brûlée its signature brittle top that will crack when you take your first spoonful. (It is not calculated in the macros.)

Note: Tagatose is a sugar alcohol similar to erythritol. It caramelizes like sugar and makes the perfect topping for crème brûlée. Do not try to caramelize erythritol or stevia because it will not work.

MACRONUTRIENTS:

| Calories: 230 | Carbs: 2.3 g | Protein: 4.3 g |
| Fat: 22.3 g | Fiber: 0 g | Net Carbs: 2.3 g |

CLASSIC CHEESECAKE

SERVES 8

PREP TIME: 30M

COOK TIME: 45M

TOTAL TIME: 1H 15M +
    6H 30M CHILL TIME

FOR CRUST:

- 1½ cups (168 g) almond flour
- 4 tablespoons (56 g) butter, melted
- 1 tablespoon (16 g) brown sugar substitute
- 1 tablespoon (12 g) granulated erythritol
- ½ teaspoon ground cinnamon
- Cooking spray

Cheesecake is the easiest keto-friendly dessert you can make when the sweet cravings attack. I used to be intimidated to make cheesecake, but it's truly so easy—maybe even easier than cake! This classic version is so decadent you will forget that it's low carb and sugar free.

To make the crust: In a medium bowl, combine the almond flour, butter, brown sugar substitute, erythritol, and cinnamon. Use a fork to press it all together. When completed, the mixture should resemble wet sand.

Spray the springform pan with cooking spray and line the bottom with parchment paper.

Press the crust evenly into the pan. Work the crust up the sides of the pan, about halfway from the top, and make sure there are no bare spots on the bottom.

Place the crust in the freezer for 20 minutes while you make the filling.

FOR FILLING:

16 ounces (454 g) cream cheese, softened

½ cup (100 g) granulated erythritol

2 eggs

1 teaspoon vanilla extract

½ teaspoon lemon extract

1½ cups (360 ml) water

ACCESSORIES NEEDED:

7" (18 cm) springform pan

Trivet

To make the filling: In the bowl of a stand mixer using the whip attachment, combine the cream cheese and erythritol on medium speed until the cream cheese is light and fluffy, 2 to 3 minutes.

Add the eggs, vanilla extract, and lemon extract. Mix until well combined.

Remove the crust from the freezer and pour in the filling. Cover the pan tightly with aluminum foil and place it on the trivet.

Add the water to the pot and carefully lower the trivet into the pot.

Close the lid and seal the vent. Cook on HIGH pressure for 45 minutes. Quick release the steam.

Remove the trivet and cheesecake from the pot. Remove the foil from the pan. The center of the cheesecake should still be slightly jiggly. If the cheesecake is still very jiggly in the center, cook for an additional 5 minutes on HIGH pressure until the appropriate doneness is reached.

Let the cheesecake cool for 30 minutes on the counter before placing it in the refrigerator to set. Leave the cheesecake in the refrigerator for at least 6 hours before removing the sides of the pan, slicing, and serving.

MACRONUTRIENTS:

Calories: 438	Carbs: 6.8 g	Protein: 10.1 g
Fat: 35.4 g	Fiber: 2.3 g	Net Carbs: 4.5 g

DOUBLE CHOCOLATE CHIP BROWNIES

SERVES 8

PREP TIME: 10M

COOK TIME: 33M

TOTAL TIME: 53M

1½ cups (168 g) almond flour

¾ cup (150 g) granulated erythritol

⅓ cup (40 g) unsweetened cocoa powder

1 teaspoon baking powder

2 eggs

1 tablespoon (15 ml) vanilla extract

5 tablespoons (70 g) butter, melted

¼ cup (44 g) sugar-free chocolate chips

Cooking spray

½ cup (120 ml) water

ACCESSORIES NEEDED:

7" (18 cm) baking dish

Trivet

Naturally, I had to include a sinfully decadent chocolate dessert in this cookbook. Let me just tell you, these brownies are one of the best recipes I've ever made, if I do say so myself. Your non-keto friends and family will be shocked to learn that there isn't a single granule of real sugar in these fudgy brownies.

In a large bowl, add the almond flour, erythritol, cocoa powder, and baking powder. Use a hand mixer on low speed to combine and smooth out any lumps.

Add the eggs and vanilla and mix until well combined.

Add the butter and mix on low speed until well combined. Scrape the bottom and sides of the bowl and mix again if needed. Fold in the chocolate chips.

Grease the baking dish with cooking spray. Pour the batter into the dish and smooth with a spatula. Cover tightly with aluminum foil.

Pour the water into the pot. Place the trivet in the pot and carefully lower the baking dish onto the trivet.

Close the lid and seal the vent. Cook on HIGH pressure for 33 minutes. Quick release the steam.

Use the handles to carefully remove the trivet from the pot. Remove the foil from the dish.

Let the brownies cool for 10 minutes before turning out onto a plate.

Note: If there is any moisture on top of the brownies, gently dab with a paper towel. Sugar-free chocolate chips can be purchased in most major grocers or online.

MACRONUTRIENTS:

Calories: 236	Carbs: 6.8 g	Protein: 6.9 g
Fat: 20.3 g	Fiber: 3.9 g	Net Carbs: 2.9 g

KENTUCKY BUTTER CAKE

SERVES 4

PREP TIME: 5M

COOK TIME: 35M

TOTAL TIME: 40M +
    COOLING TIME

2 cups (224 g) almond
    flour

¾ cup (150 g) granulated
    erythritol

1½ teaspoons baking
    powder

4 eggs

1 tablespoon (15 ml)
    vanilla extract

½ cup (112 g) butter,
    melted

Cooking spray

½ cup (120 ml) water

ACCESSORIES NEEDED:

7" (18 cm) Bundt pan

Trivet

I'm not sure how Kentucky Butter Cake earned its name, but because I live in Kentucky these days, I thought it only appropriate to include an Instant Pot version in this book. Butter cake is a simple but rich golden yellow cake. This recipe is my go-to for birthday cakes, too.

In a medium bowl, whisk together the almond flour, erythritol, and baking powder. Whisk well to remove any lumps.

Add the eggs and vanilla and whisk until combined.

Add the butter and whisk until the batter is mostly smooth and well combined.

Grease the pan with cooking spray and pour in the batter. Cover tightly with aluminum foil.

Add the water to the pot. Place the Bundt pan on the trivet and carefully lower it into the pot using.

Close the lid and seal the vent. Cook on HIGH pressure for 35 minutes. Quick release the steam.

Remove the pan from the pot. Let the cake cool in the pan before flipping out onto a plate.

Note: Make a glaze for the cake by following the directions for the Cinnamon Roll Coffee Cake on page 42. This is not calculated in the macros.

MACRONUTRIENTS:

Calories: 180	Carbs: 2 g	Protein: 2 g
Fat: 16 g	Fiber: 0 g	Net Carbs: 2 g

SALTED CARAMEL PUMPKIN CHEESECAKE

SERVES 8

PREP TIME: 30M

COOK TIME: 45M

TOTAL TIME: 1H 15M +
6H 30M CHILL TIME

FOR CRUST:

1½ cups (168 g) almond flour

4 tablespoons (56 g) butter, melted

1 tablespoon (16 g) brown sugar substitute

1 tablespoon (12 g) granulated erythritol

½ teaspoon ground cinnamon

Cooking spray

FOR FILLING:

16 ounces (454 g) cream cheese, softened

½ cup (100 g) granulated erythritol

2 eggs

¼ cup (60 g) pumpkin puree (not pumpkin pie filling)

3 tablespoons (45 ml) sugar-free salted caramel syrup (see Note)

1 teaspoon vanilla extract

¼ teaspoon pumpkin pie spice

1½ cups (360 ml) water

I'm not a fan of drinking pumpkin-spice beverages, but I sure love eating pumpkin-spiced foods! This pumpkin cheesecake is ultra creamy, slightly pumpkin-y, and very caramel-y. (Those are highly technical culinary terms, by the way.) Making cheesecake in the Instant Pot is the best way because you don't have to babysit the oven. Just set it and forget it! Trust me when I say, you don't want to wait until autumn to make this cheesecake.

To make the crust: In a medium bowl, combine the almond flour, butter, brown sugar substitute, erythritol, and cinnamon. Use a fork to press it all together. When completed, the mixture should resemble wet sand.

Spray the pan with cooking spray and line the bottom with parchment paper.

Press the crust evenly into the pan. Work the crust up the sides of the pan, about halfway from the top, and make sure there are no bare spots on the bottom.

Place the crust in the freezer for 20 minutes while you make the filling.

To make the filling: In a large bowl using a hand mixer on medium speed, combine the cream cheese and erythritol. Beat until the cream cheese is light and fluffy, 2 to 3 minutes.

Add the eggs, pumpkin puree, caramel syrup, vanilla, and pumpkin pie spice. Beat until well combined.

Remove the crust from the freezer and pour in the filling. Cover the pan with aluminum foil and place it on the trivet.

Add the water to the pot and carefully lower the trivet into the pot.

Close the lid and seal the vent. Cook on HIGH pressure for 45 minutes. Quick release the steam.

Remove the trivet and cheesecake from the pot. Remove the foil from the pan. The center of the cheesecake should still be slightly jiggly. If the

7" (18 cm) springform pan

Trivet

cheesecake is still very jiggly in the center, cook for an additional 5 minutes on HIGH pressure or until the appropriate doneness is reached.

Let the cheesecake cool for 30 minutes on the counter before placing it in the refrigerator to set. Leave the cheesecake in the refrigerator for at least 6 hours before removing the sides and serving.

Note: Salted caramel syrup can be found at many major grocery stores. You can usually find flavored syrups in the coffee aisle.

MACRONUTRIENTS:

Calories: 408
Fat: 35.9 g

Carbs: 6.8 g
Fiber: 2.5 g

Protein: 10.2 g
Net Carbs: 4.3 g

SOUTHERN SUGAR PIE

SERVES 12

PREP TIME: 5M

COOK TIME: 35M

TOTAL TIME: 40M +
    COOLING TIME

2 cups (224 g) almond
    flour

1½ cups (288 g) powdered
    erythritol

1 teaspoon baking
    powder

Pinch of salt

½ cup (120 g) sour cream

4 tablespoons (56 g)
    butter, melted

1 egg

1 teaspoon vanilla extract

Cooking spray

1½ teaspoons ground
    cinnamon

1½ teaspoons brown
    sugar substitute

1 cup (240 ml) water

ACCESSORIES NEEDED:

7" (18 cm) baking dish

Trivet

One of my family's favorite desserts used to be a little thing called sugar pie. It was similar to chess pie but less buttery and sweeter. While I was writing this book, one of my recipe tests did not come out as I expected. Instead, I was left with this buttery, sweet, and creamy slice of happiness. Top a slice with a dollop of fresh whipped cream and a few tart berries.

In a large bowl, whisk together the almond flour, powdered erythritol, baking powder, and salt.

Add the sour cream, butter, egg, and vanilla and whisk until well combined. The batter will be very thick, almost like cookie dough.

Grease the baking dish with cooking spray. Line with parchment paper, if desired.

Transfer the batter to the dish and level with an offset spatula.

In a small bowl, combine the cinnamon and brown sugar substitute. Sprinkle over the top of the batter. You may swirl the mixture through the batter, if desired.

Cover the dish tightly with aluminum foil. Add the water to the pot. Set the dish on the trivet and carefully lower it into the pot.

Close the lid and seal the vent. Cook on HIGH pressure for 35 minutes. Quick release the steam.

Remove the trivet and pie from the pot. Remove the foil from the pan. The pie should be set but soft, and the top should be slightly cracked.

Cool completely before cutting.

Note: This "pie" will form somewhat of its own crust upon cooling. If you don't have powdered erythritol, pulse granulated erythritol through a food processor a few times.

MACRONUTRIENTS:

| Calories: 222 | Carbs: 4.9 g | Protein: 5.5 g |
| Fat: 19.1 g | Fiber: 2.3 g | Net Carbs: 2.7 g |

Resources

FURTHER READING

Low Carb Implications

www.ruled.me/new-major-study-on-low-carb-implications

A Ketogenic Diet for Beginners

www.dietdoctor.com/low-carb/keto

KetoDiet Nutrition and Exercise: Protein

ketodietapp.com/Blog/lchf/ketogenic-nutrition-and-exercise-protein

Bodybuilding on the Ketogenic Diet

www.ruled.me/comprehensive-guide-bodybuilding-ketogenic-diet

NUTRITIONAL INFORMATION

USDA Food Composition Database

ndb.nal.usda.gov/ndb/nutrients/index

Acknowledgments

Wow, I wrote a cookbook! Never in my dreamiest of dreams would I have thought little 'ol me would write a cookbook. When I signed the contract to begin this book, I was as terrified as I was excited. By no coincidence, I was blessed with a phenomenal support team that any author would feel privileged to walk alongside.

First, I want to thank God for whispering "trust me" and sending me down this path of writing, blogging, and connecting with the world. You opened doors for me that I did not know existed and showed me what walking in my faith truly means. None of this would matter without you. I don't deserve any of your blessings, but I am eternally grateful.

To my family: Thank you for encouraging me, supporting me, and celebrating with me when I wanted to start a "little blog." Thank you to my husband, *Jonathan*, for pulling extra weight with the kiddos so I could write in quiet and for supporting me to chase this dream! Thank you to *my parents* for always believing in me and teaching me from a young age that I am capable of doing anything I put my mind to. Thank you to *my children*, who love me unconditionally and are always the first to jump up and down to celebrate with me—even when they have no clue what we're celebrating. I love you all so incredibly much!

To my rockstar publishing team, *Jill Alexander, Meredith Quinn, David Martinell,* and *Jennifer Kushnier*: Y'all are the real MVPs!

Jill, thank you for taking a chance on me. You talked me off the ledge more times than I'd like to admit, calmed my nerves when I didn't understand the process, and truly carried me through this book-writing process like a gazelle. Your poise and grace did not go unnoticed and it has been a true honor to work with you.

Meredith, thank you for helping me see the light at the end of the tunnel and for helping me cross the finish line gracefully. Your finesse was like the final seasoning needed to make this book shine! You were a delight to work alongside.

David, thank you for caring so much about the design, look, and feel of this book. You probably had the hardest job of anyone: working on design with a very particular and very opinionated author. Ha! Thank you for listening to all of my ideas, likes, and dislikes and working so hard to make sure I loved every aspect of the book. Your tenacity to make this book beautiful is evident to all with each turn of the page.

Jennifer, bless your heart girl, you GOT me! Thank you for making the daunting task of editing my work painless and fun. I genuinely enjoyed reading your comments and jokes throughout the editing process.

To my friends, *Natalie, Crystal, Lauren, Melanie, Allie,* and *Lauren Ashley:* Your friendship, support, and love have carried me through this process more than you know! I am so grateful for all of you and love you all.

To *Amy, Lisa, Morgan, Amanda,* and *Julie,* my Cincy Keto Queens! To think this little thing called keto brought us all together is just crazy. You ladies are some of the best friends a girl could ask for.

And last, but certainly not least, I want to think my *Keto In Pearls* community. To all of you who have subscribed to my emails, made my recipes, or followed me on Instagram: This book is for you! You have no idea how much joy I feel when you tell me your children, co-workers, friends, or spouse loved one of my recipes. I am so thankful God gave me a gift that I get to use by serving all of you! Without y'all, and God, none of this would be possible!

About the Author

Anna Hunley is the chief recipe curator at the popular lifestyle blog *Keto in Pearls*. Born and raised in Atlanta, Georgia, she now resides in northern Kentucky. Anna began blogging in 2017 as a hobby while she learned how to cook for a ketogenic lifestyle. Her blog is now one of the most visited blogs in the keto community, beloved for her accessible, kid-tested, family-approved recipes.

Photo Credit: Natalie Morgan

Index

A

Alfredo sauce, in Spaghetti Squash Alfredo, 168
Almond flour, 23
  Chocolate Cake with Whipped Chocolate Frosting, 178–179
  Cinnamon Roll Coffee Cake, 42
  Classic Cheesecake, 182–183
  Double Chocolate Chip Brownies, 185
  Fat Head Dough, 18
  Kentucky Butter Cake, 186
  Maple Bacon Corn Bread, 165
  Salted Caramel Pumpkin Cheesecake, 188–189
  Southern "Corn Bread" Dressing, 166
  Southern Sugar Pie, 191
  Two-Bite Pancakes, 38
Arrowroot powder, 23
Asparagus
  Asparagus and Gruyère Frittata, 36
  carbohydrates in, 16
Avocado oil, 23

B

Bacon
  Bacon and Cheddar–Stuffed Burgers, 96
  Bacon and Cream Cheese–Stuffed Chicken with Bacon Gravy, 119
  Bacon Jelly, 156
  Cauliflower and Bacon Chowder, 63
  Garlic-Parmesan Chicken Wings, 52
  Kentucky Hot Brown Casserole, 83
  Millionaire Cheese Dip, 52
  Southern-Style Green Beans, 167
  Spaghetti Squash Alfredo, 168
Bacon bits
  Maple Bacon Corn Bread, 65
  Pimento Cheese Crack Chicken, 137
  Twice-Baked Mashed Cauliflower, 173
Baking dish, Instant Pot, 29
Basil (fresh)
  Cod Fillets with Basil Butter, 124
  Goat Cheese and Bruschetta–Stuffed Chicken, 122
BBQ Glaze, Baby Back Ribs with, 95

BBQ sauce (sugar-free)
  Game Day Meatballs, 50
  Georgia Brunswick Stew, 73
  Un-Sloppy Joes, 107
Beef. See also Chuck roast; Ground beef
  Baby Back Ribs with BBQ Glaze, 95
  Beef Tenderloin with Red Wine Reduction, 99
  Carne Asada Bites, 100
  1-Minute Breakfast Steak, 35
  Philly Cheesesteak–Stuffed Peppers, 106
  Red Wine Beef Stew, 74
  Shredded Beef, 92
  Take-Out Style Beef and Broccoli, 97
Beef marrow bones, in Bone Broth, 93
Beer, in Salsa Verde Carnitas, 141
Bell pepper
  carbohydrates in, 16
  Chicken Fajitas, 121
  Chicken Ro-Tel, 79
  First Place Chili, 69
  Philly Cheesesteak–Stuffed Peppers, 106
  Pizza-Stuffed Chicken, 151
  Shrimp Étouffée, 146
  Taco Soup, 71
Blackberry jam, in Game Day Meatballs, 50
Black tea, in Zero-Calorie Southern Sweet Tea, 57
Bone Broth, 93
Bourbon, in Maple-Bourbon Salmon, 134
Broccoli
  Broccoli-Cheddar Egg Bites, 41
  Broccoli-Cheddar Soup, 60
  Broccoli with Garlic-Herb Cheese Sauce, 158
  carbohydrates in, 16
  Spinach Artichoke Chicken Casserole, 88
  Take-Out Style Beef and Broccoli, 97
Brownies, Double Chocolate Chip, 185
Brown sugar substitute, 21, 23
Brussels sprouts, carbohydrates in, 16

Buffalo wing sauce
  Buffalo Chicken Meatballs, 42
  Chicken Wing Dip, 54
Bundt pan, Instant Pot, 29
Burgers
  Bacon and Cheddar–Stuffed Burgers, 96
  Chili-Lime Turkey Burgers with Sriracha-Lime Dipping Sauce, 123

C

Cabbage, carbohydrates in, 16
Cakes
  Chocolate Cake with Whipped Chocolate Frosting, 178–179
  Classic Cheesecake, 182–183
  Kentucky Butter Cake, 186
  Salted Caramel Pumpkin Cheesecake, 188–189
Calories, in a ketogenic diet, 13
Capers, in Salmon Fillets with Lemon-Dill Butter, 143
Caramel syrup (sugar-free), in Salted Caramel Pumpkin Cheesecake, 188–189
Carbohydrates, 12–13, 15–16, 17
Carnitas, Salsa Verde. See Salsa Verde Carnitas
Carrots
  Broccoli-Cheddar Soup, 60
  Chicken Zoodle Soup, 64
  Crustless Chicken Pot Pie, 89
  Red Wine Beef Stew, 74
  Shrimp Étouffée, 146
  Sweet Country Carrots, 171
Cauliflower
  carbohydrates in, 16
  Cauliflower and Bacon Chowder, 63
  Cheesy Chicken and Cauliflower Rice, 78
  Chicken Ro-Tel, 79
  Faux Mac and Cheese, 161
  Horseradish Whipped Cauliflower, 162
  Mexican Cauliflower Rice, 20
  Twice-Baked Mashed Cauliflower, 173

Cauliflower rice
Cheesy Chicken and Cauliflower
Rice, 78
Deconstructed Egg Rolls with Peanut
Sauce, 81–82
Mexican Cauliflower Rice, 20
Cheese. *See also* Cream cheese
cheddar cheese
Bacon and Cheddar–Stuffed
Burgers, 96
Broccoli-Cheddar Egg Bites, 41
Broccoli-Cheddar Soup, 60
Broccoli with Garlic-Herb Cheese
Sauce, 158
Faux Mac and Cheese, 161
Garlic-Parmesan Chicken Wings, 52
Kentucky Hot Brown Casserole, 83
Pimento Cheese Dip, 55
Twice-Baked Mashed Cauliflower, 173
feta, in Greek Chicken, 130
garlic and herb spread, in Broccoli with
Garlic-Herb Cheese Sauce, 158
Gruyère cheese
Asparagus and Gruyère Frittata, 36
French Onion Soup, 70
Mexican cheese blend, in Enchilada
Casserole, 85
mozzarella cheese
Deep-Dish Pizza Dip, 48
Fat Head Dough, 18
on Italian Meatloaf, 105
Parmesan cheese
Bacon and Cream Cheese–Stuffed
Chicken with Bacon Gravy, 119
Baked Pizza Eggs, 39
Creamed Spinach, 157
Garlic-Parmesan Chicken Wings, 51
Italian Meatloaf, 103
Lemon Chicken, 133
Spaghetti Squash Alfredo, 168
Spinach Artichoke Chicken
Casserole, 88
processed yellow melting cheese
Cheesy Chicken and Cauliflower
Rice, 78
Chicken Ro-Tel, 79
Queso Fundido, 56

provolone cheese
Philly Cheesesteak–Stuffed
Peppers, 106
Pizza-Stuffed Chicken, 151
ricotta, in Deep-Dish Pizza Dip, 48
Cheesecake
Classic Cheesecake, 182–183
Salted Caramel Pumpkin Cheese-
cake, 188–189
Chicken. *See also* Roast Chicken
Bacon and Cream Cheese–Stuffed
Chicken with Bacon Gravy, 119
Buffalo Chicken Meatballs, 47
Cheesy Chicken and Cauliflower
Rice, 78
Chicken Fajitas, 121
Chicken Ro-Tel, 79
Chicken Wing Dip, 54
Chicken with Spinach and Sun-Dried
Tomatoes, 120
Chicken Zoodle Soup, 64
Crispy Chicken Thighs with Gravy, 129
Garlic-Parmesan Chicken Wings, 51
Georgia Brunswick Stew, 73
Goat Cheese and Bruschetta–Stuffed
Chicken, 122
Greek Chicken, 130
Kentucky Hot Brown Casserole, 83
Lemon Chicken, 133
Pizza-Stuffed Chicken, 151
Shredded Chicken, 114
Take-Out Style Orange Chicken, 145
Teriyaki Chicken, 150
Children, ketogenic diet for, 21–22
Chili
Cincinnati-Style Chili, 61
Creamy Green Chile and Carnitas
Chili, 68
First Place Chili, 69
Chipotle peppers, in Carne Asada
Bites, 100
Chocolate chips (sugar-free), in Double
Chocolate Chip Brownies, 185
Chorizo, in Queso Fundido, 56
Chowder, Cauliflower and Bacon, 63
Chuck roast
French Dip Roast Beef, 101
Italian Pot Roast with Giardiniera
Gravy, 104
Sunday Pot Roast, 110

Cilantro
Carne Asada Bites, 100
Chili-Lime Turkey Burgers with Sriracha-Lime Dipping Sauce, 123
Cinnamon Roll Coffee Cake, 42
Cocoa powder
Chocolate Cake with Whipped Chocolate Frosting, 178–179
Cincinnati-Style Chili, 61
Double Chocolate Chip Brownies, 185
Coconut aminos
Deconstructed Egg Rolls with Peanut
Sauce, 81–82
Sticky Country Ribs, 149
Take-Out Style Beef and Broccoli, 97
Take-Out Style Orange Chicken, 145
Teriyaki Chicken, 150
Coconut oil, 23
Coffee Cake, Cinnamon Roll, 42
Coffee, in Chocolate Cake with
Whipped Chocolate Frosting,
178–179
Coleslaw mix, in Deconstructed Egg
Rolls with Peanut Sauce, 81–82
"Corn Bread" Dressing, 166
Corn Bread, Maple Bacon, 165
Crab boil seasoning
Millionaire Cheese Dip, 52
Shrimp Étouffée, 146
Crab Legs, No-Boil, 136
Cream cheese
Bacon and Cream Cheese–Stuffed
Chicken with Bacon Gravy, 119
Cauliflower and Bacon Chowder, 63
Cheesy Chicken and Cauliflower
Rice, 78
Chicken Wing Dip, 54
Chicken with Spinach and Sun-Dried
Tomatoes, 120
Chocolate Cake with Whipped Chocolate Frosting, 178
Cinnamon Roll Coffee Cake, 42
Classic Cheesecake, 182–183
Cod Fillets with Basil Butter, 124
Creamed Spinach, 157
Creamy Green Chile and Carnitas
Chili, 68
Deep-Dish Pizza Dip, 48
Faux Mac and Cheese, 161
Garlic-Parmesan Chicken Wings, 52
Homemade Cream of Chicken Soup, 67

Homemade Egg Noodles, 19
Kentucky Hot Brown Casserole, 83
Lemon Chicken, 133
Millionaire Cheese, 52
Pimento Cheese Crack Chicken, 137
Pizza-Stuffed Chicken, 151
Queso Fundido, 56
Salted Caramel Pumpkin Cheese-
   cake, 188–189
Twice-Baked Mashed Cauliflower, 173
Crème Brûlée, 180–181
Cucumber, in Greek Chicken, 130

D
Dips
   Chicken Wing Dip, 54
   Deep-Dish Pizza Dip, 48
   Millionaire Cheese Dip, 52
   Pimento Cheese Dip, 55

E
Egg mold, Instant Pot, 30
Egg Noodles, Homemade, 19
Eggplant, 16
Eggs
   Asparagus and Gruyère Frittata, 36
   Baked Pizza Eggs, 39
   Broccoli-Cheddar Egg Bites, 41
   carbohydrates in, 16
   Crème Brûlée, 180–181
   Homemade Egg Noodles, 19
   No-Peel Hard-Boiled Eggs, 34
Enchilada sauce, in Enchilada
   Casserole, 85
Erythritol, 23
   about, 21
   Chicken Fajitas, 121
   Chocolate Cake with Whipped Choc-
      olate Frosting, 178
   Cinnamon Roll Coffee Cake, 42
   Classic Cheesecake, 182–183
   Crème Brûlée, 180–181
   Double Chocolate Chip Brownies, 185
   Easy Marinara Sauce, 160
   Kentucky Butter Cake, 186
   Maple Bacon Corn Bread, 165
   Salted Caramel Pumpkin Cheese-
      cake, 188–189
   Southern Sugar Pie, 191
   Take-Out Style Beef and Broccoli, 97
   Take-Out Style Orange Chicken, 145

Two-Bite Pancakes, 38
Zero-Calorie Southern Sweet Tea, 57

F
Fat Head Dough, 18
Fats, 12–14
Fish and seafood
   Cod Fillets with Basil Butter, 124
   Easy Lobster Tails, 125
   Maple-Bourbon Salmon, 134
   No-Boil Crab Legs, 136
   Salmon Fillets with Lemon-Dill
      Butter, 143
   Shrimp Étouffée, 146

G
Garlic, Roasted, 155
Giardiniera mix, in Italian Pot Roast
   with Giardiniera Gravy, 104
Ginger
   Deconstructed Egg Rolls with Peanut
      Sauce, 81
   Take-Out Style Beef and Broccoli, 97
   Teriyaki Chicken, 150
   Goat Cheese and Bruschetta–Stuffed
      Chicken, 122
Green beans
   carbohydrates in, 16
   Crustless Chicken Pot Pie, 89
   Southern-Style Green Beans, 167
Green chiles, in Shrimp Étouffée, 146
Green chili salsa, in Creamy Green
   Chile and Carnitas Chili, 68
Green peas
   Chicken Ro-Tel, 79
   Red Wine Beef Stew, 74
   Spaghetti Squash Alfredo, 168
Ground beef
   Bacon and Cheddar–Stuffed Burgers, 96
   Beef Stroganoff Meatballs, 98
   Cincinnati-Style Chili, 61
   Enchilada Casserole, 85
   First Place Chili, 69
   Italian Meatloaf, 103
   Salisbury Steak, 109
   Taco Soup, 71
   Un-Sloppy Joes, 107
Ground pork, in Deconstructed Egg
   Rolls with Peanut Sauce, 81–82

H
Ham, Holiday Spiral, 131
Heavy cream
   Asparagus and Gruyère Frittata, 36
   Beef Stroganoff Meatballs, 98
   Broccoli-Cheddar Egg Bites, 41
   Broccoli-Cheddar Soup, 60
   Broccoli with Garlic-Herb Cheese
      Sauce, 158
   Cauliflower and Bacon Chowder, 63
   Cheesy Chicken and Cauliflower
      Rice, 78
   Cod Fillets with Basil Butter, 124
   Creamed Spinach, 157
   Creamy Green Chile and Carnitas
      Chili, 68
   Crème Brûlée, 180–181
   Crispy Chicken Thighs with Gravy, 129
   Crustless Chicken Pot Pie, 89
   Faux Mac and Cheese, 161
   Homemade Cream of Chicken Soup, 67
   Horseradish Whipped Cauliflower, 162
   Kentucky Hot Brown Casserole, 83
   Lemon Chicken, 133
   Pimento Cheese Dip, 55
   Pork Chops with Maple-Dijon Cream
      Sauce, 138
   Queso Fundido, 56
Homemade Cream of Chicken Soup
   Poppy Seed Chicken, 86
   recipe, 67
Horseradish Whipped Cauliflower, 162

I
Instant Pot
   about, 28–29
   accessories for, 29–30
   care of, 31
   cook times, 29

J
Jalapeño, in Taco Soup, 71

K
Kale, carbohydrates in, 16
Keto flu, avoiding, 13
Ketogenic diet
   author's experience with, 8
   calories in, 13
   for children, 21–22
   as family friendly, 8–9

foods eaten with a, 13–17
foods forbidden with, 17
history of, 11
macro requirements, 12–13
meal plans, 24–25
nutritional ketosis and, 12
shopping for, 22–24
three main components of, 12
Keto in Pearls blog, 8
Ketones, 12

L

Lemon
   Cod Fillets with Basil Butter, 124
   Lemon Chicken, 133
   Salmon Fillets with Lemon-Dill
      Butter, 143
Lettuce, carbohydrates in, 16
Leucine, 14
Limes
   Carne Asada Bites, 100
   Chili-Lime Turkey Burgers with
      Sriracha-Lime Dipping Sauce,
      123
Liquid smoke
   Baby Back Ribs with BBQ Glaze, 95
   Bacon and Cheddar–Stuffed Burgers, 96
Lobster tails, 125

M

Macronutrients (macros), 12–13, 13–14
Maple syrup (sugar-free)
   Baby Back Ribs with BBQ Glaze, 95
   Bacon Jelly, 156
   Candied Pecans, 177
   Deconstructed Egg Rolls with Peanut
      Sauce, 81–82
   Holiday Spiral Ham, 131
   Maple Bacon Corn Bread, 65
   Maple-Bourbon Salmon, 134
   Pork Chops with Maple-Dijon Cream
      Sauce, 138
   Spaghetti Squash Alfredo, 171
   Sweet Country Carrots, 171
Marinara sauce
   Baked Pizza Eggs, 39
   Deep-Dish Pizza Dip, 48
   Easy Marinara Sauce, 160
   Pizza-Stuffed Chicken, 151
Meal plans, 24–25

Meatballs
   Buffalo Chicken Meatballs, 47
   Game Day Meatballs, 50
Meatloaf, Italian, 103
Migraines, 12
Monk fruit, 21
Muscle, building, 14
Mushrooms
   Beef Stroganoff Meatballs, 98
   carbohydrates in, 16
   Chicken Ro-Tel, 79
   Philly Cheesesteak–Stuffed Peppers, 106
   Pork Chops with Maple-Dijon Cream
      Sauce, 138
   Red Wine Beef Stew, 74
   Rosemary Mushrooms, 163
   Salisbury Steak, 109

N

Noodles, Homemade Egg, 19

O

Okra, in Shrimp Étouffée, 146
Olives, in Greek Chicken, 130
Onions
   carbohydrates in, 16
   French Onion Soup, 70
   Sweet Onion Relish, 172

P

Pancakes, Two-Bite, 38
Pancetta, in Spaghetti Squash Alfredo,
   168
Parsley (fresh)
   Beef Stroganoff Meatballs, 98
   Pork Tenderloin Medallions with Pan
      Sauce, 140
Peanut butter, in Deconstructed Egg
   Rolls with Peanut Sauce, 81–82
Pecans
   Candied Pecans, 177
   Maple-Bourbon Salmon, 134
Pepperoni
   Deep-Dish Pizza Dip, 48
   Pizza-Stuffed Chicken, 151
Pies
   Crustless Chicken Pot Pie, 89
   Southern Sugar Pie, 191
Pimento Cheese Dip
   Pimento Cheese Crack Chicken, 137
   recipe, 55

Pork. *See also* Bacon
   Coffee-Rubbed Pulled Pork, 126
   Deconstructed Egg Rolls with Peanut
      Sauce, 81–82
   Georgia Brunswick Stew, 73
   Holiday Spiral Ham, 131
   Pork Chops with Maple-Dijon Cream
      Sauce, 138
   Pork Tenderloin Medallions with Pan
      Sauce, 140
   Salsa Verde Carnitas, 141
   Sauerkraut Pork Roast, 144
   Sticky Country Ribs, 149
Pork rinds
   Italian Meatloaf, 103
   Poppy Seed Chicken, 86
Potassium, 13
Pot Roast, Sunday, 110
Processed foods, 7, 15
Proteins, 12–13
Pumpkin puree, in Salted Caramel
      Pumpkin Cheesecake, 188–189

R

Radishes
   Broccoli-Cheddar Soup, 60
   carbohydrates in, 16
   Red Wine Beef Stew, 74
   Sunday Pot Roast, 110
Ranch dressing, in Chicken Wing Dip, 54
Red wine
   Beef Tenderloin with Red Wine
      Reduction, 99
   Red Wine Beef Stew, 74
   Rosemary Mushrooms, 163
Relish, Sweet Onion, 172
Roast Chicken
   Crustless Chicken Pot Pie, 89
   Pimento Cheese Crack Chicken, 137
   Poppy Seed Chicken, 86
   recipe, 115
   Spinach Artichoke Chicken
      Casserole, 88
Roasted Garlic
   Easy Marinara Sauce, 160
   recipe, 155

S

Salmon
  Maple-Bourbon Salmon, 134
  Salmon Fillets with Lemon-Dill
    Butter, 143
Salsa Verde Carnitas
  Creamy Green Chile and Carnitas
    Chili, 68
  recipe, 141
Sauerkraut, in Sauerkraut Pork Roast, 144
Sausage, in Queso Fundido, 56
Sazón Goya seasoning, in Mexican
    Cauliflower Rice, 20
Sealing ring, Instant Pot, 30
Shopping, 22–24
Shredded Beef, 92
Shredded Chicken
  Cheesy Chicken and Cauliflower
    Rice, 78
  recipe, 114
Shrimp
  Millionaire Cheese Dip, 52
  Shrimp Étouffée, 146
Sodium, 13
Soups
  Broccoli-Cheddar Soup, 60
  Chicken Zoodle Soup, 64
  French Onion Soup, 70
  Homemade Cream of Chicken Soup, 67
  Taco Soup, 71
Sour cream
  Beef Stroganoff Meatballs, 98
  Chicken with Spinach and Sun-Dried
    Tomatoes, 120
  Chili-Lime Turkey Burgers with Srira-
    cha-Lime Dipping Sauce, 123
  Cinnamon Roll Coffee Cake, 42
  Enchilada Casserole, 85
  Greek Chicken, 130
  Horseradish Whipped Cauliflower, 162
  Poppy Seed Chicken, 86
  Southern Sugar Pie, 191
Spaghetti squash
  carbohydrates in, 16
  Spaghetti Squash Alfredo, 168
Spinach
  carbohydrates in, 16
  Chicken with Spinach and Sun-Dried
    Tomatoes, 120
  Creamed Spinach, 157

Spinach artichoke dip, in Spinach
    Artichoke Chicken Casserole, 88
Springform pan, Instant Pot, 29
Squash, in Spaghetti Squash Alfredo, 168
Steamer basket, Instant Pot, 30
Stevia, 21
Stews
  Georgia Brunswick Stew, 73
  Red Wine Beef Stew, 74
Strawberry jelly (sugar-free), in Sticky
    Country Ribs, 149
Sugar alcohols, 15, 21
Sugar-free sports drinks, 13
Sugar, keto sweeteners replacing, 21
Sun-dried tomatoes, in Chicken with
    Spinach and Sun-Dried Tomatoes, 120
Sweeteners, keto, 21–22

T

Tagatose, in Crème Brûlée, 180–181
Tea, Zero-Calorie Southern Sweet, 57
Tomatoes (canned)
  Chicken Ro-Tel, 79
  Cincinnati-Style Chili, 61
  Easy Marinara Sauce, 160
  First Place Chili, 69
  Georgia Brunswick Stew, 73
  Mexican Cauliflower Rice, 20
  Queso Fundido, 56
  Shrimp Étouffée, 146
  Taco Soup, 71
Tomatoes (fresh)
  Asparagus and Gruyère Frittata, 36
  Goat Cheese and Bruschetta–Stuffed
    Chicken, 122
  Greek Chicken, 130
  Kentucky Hot Brown Casserole, 83
Tortillas, in Enchilada Casserole, 85
Trivet, Instant Pot, 29
Turkey
  Anytime Thanksgiving Turkey,
    116–117
  ground, in Chili-Lime Turkey Burgers
    with Sriracha-Lime Dipping
    Sauce, 123
  Kentucky Hot Brown Casserole, 83

U

U.S. Department of Agriculture (USDA)
    Food Composition Database, 12

W

Water intake, 13
Weight gain, 7–8
Weight loss, 12
Whiskey, in Maple-Bourbon Salmon, 134

X

Xanthan gum, 23
Xylitol, 21

Y

Yellow melting cheese. *See* Cheese,
    processed yellow melting cheese

Z

Zucchini
  carbohydrates in, 16
  Chicken Zoodle Soup, 64
  tortillas substituted with, 85